ADDITIONAL COMMENTS ABOUT THIS BOOK

"*Creating a Happier Life* by David Lindsey is just what the author tells us it is--a manual for personal transformation. For those who are ready and willing to change, this book will be a big help."

> Dr. Bernie S. Siegel
> New Haven, CT

"If you want to make dramatic changes in your life, you can best learn how from someone who has done it. Dr. David Lindsey is such a person. He has searched, found, and practiced success principles and as a result, he has transformed his own life. He has created new dimensions of personal happiness, peace, and prosperity. With great enthusiasm I endorse Dr. David Lindsey's book *Creating a Happier Life*."

> Mike Wickett
> Birmingham, MI

"Through inspirational material and practical message, *Creating a Happier Life* empowers the individual to make tremendous strides in personal growth. This book also provides deep insight into the development of the human soul."

> Rev. Laura Maday
> Flint, Michigan

D1157778

Creating a

Happier Life

By

David M. Lindsey, Ph.D.

A MANUAL FOR PERSONAL TRANSFORMATION

First printing June, 1990

Published by:
Personal Growth Institute
2638 Browning Ave.
Lake Orion, Michigan 48360

ISBN 1-878040-00-6

Printed in the United States of America

Dedication

**To my wonderful wife, Gail, whose loving
support has made this book possible.**

Acknowledgments

I wish to express my deepest gratitude to my Higher Power, the God within, for providing the information for this book.

I also wish to express gratitude to Rev. Jack Boland for helping me discover that I have a Higher Power.

A very special thanks to my family and friends who supported me during the writing and publication of this book. I'm particularly grateful to my wife, Gail, for her many invaluable suggestions and contributions; to Maureen McDonald, Sonia Foster, and Tanya Rowland for their editorial support; to Larry Tucci for his creative cover design; and to Anjali Nanda of Graphic Ideas for her assistance in the publication.

DML

CONTENTS

—Day #1—

Program overview

Welcome to a personal transformation program that is guaranteed to make you a happier person. Welcome to a program that is based on practical applications of spiritual knowledge, as well as proven, rational concepts. Welcome to a program that has in the past year enhanced thousands of lives. Welcome to a personal transformation program that will help **you** create a happier life.

There are only two prerequisites for this program. The first is honesty. If you are completely honest with yourself as you read this book, major awarenesses will occur. You will learn a great deal about who you really are and why your personality has developed the way it has. You will become aware of the reasons you react the way you do in stressful situations. You will also discover which relationships in your life are really important to you, and which ones should be dissolved. Through an honest evaluation of yourself, you will develop a deeper relationship with your Higher Power, the God within.

The second prerequisite for this program is an open mind. It's very difficult for most of us to open our minds to new ways of thinking. It took me over 40 years before I was willing to accept the information that is presented in this program. But, when I finally did, my life changed, and I became a much happier person.

Usually it takes a major tragedy such as a serious illness, a divorce, or a death of a loved one, before we realize that our current thoughts and beliefs are inadequate to sustain happy lives. Too often, it's not until one of these "disasters" has occurred that we are willing to open our minds to new concepts. Are you ready for some new thoughts about life? If so, you will gain a great deal of knowledge and inner peace from this program. And with this knowledge, you will become a much happier person. Life was meant to be happy. It's only when we are unwilling to learn life's lessons that we become unhappy.

Life was meant to be happy. It's only when we are unwilling to learn life's lessons that we become unhappy.

Program description

There are three parts to this 15-day program. The first part is *"Spiritual Knowledge."* In this section, many spiritual beliefs from throughout the world are presented. Although most of the beliefs are directly from the Christian religion, some are not. Some beliefs are from the New Age movement, and some are from the Eastern religions. You will be encouraged to accept whatever beliefs intuitively feel right to you. This is an area where the heart must be open. Your first reaction may be to reject some of the beliefs presented, because you were not taught such doctrine as a child. Whatever you accept as being true will be exactly right for you. We are all on unique spiritual paths that lead to the same final destination.

The second part of this program is *"Self-Awareness."* This section has been designed to help you obtain a more thorough understanding of yourself. In this part you'll be required to answer many important questions about yourself and your relationships with others. This section is considered by many to be the most difficult, because it often resurfaces unresolved negative feelings that have been buried deep within the subconscious mind. This part of the program, however, is very important for the success of your personal transformation.

The third part of this program is considered by many to be the most helpful on a daily basis. It's called *"Practical Applications of Spiritual Knowledge."* Some of the subjects addressed in this section are forgiveness, self-esteem, inner peace, Christian meditation, and positive attitudes. Although each of these subjects is discussed from a spiritual viewpoint, the information is extremely useful. Many people have reported back to me that the information in this section of the program has greatly changed their lives.

Before you start this program, I would like to make two suggestions. The first is that you read only one chapter per day. And the second is that you take time to complete the *"Follow-up Exercises"* at the end of each chapter. The reason I make these suggestions is because the people who have been involved with this program have found that there is greater comprehension of the material if the information is presented over a two week period, and if the follow-up exercises are completed. Some people even believe that doing the follow-up exercises is just as important as reading the text.

If you are expecting a personal miracle to occur as you read this book, I have some great news for you. It will!

If you believe in miracles, miracles will occur.

Author's "rocky road" to happiness

Many authors have written books about subjects they understand from reading other books. Some authors have written books based on their own personal experiences. Usually, when I read a self-help book, I prefer to read one in which the author has "walked the talk." I find a book more credible if the author has experienced the subject first hand. For one reason or another, I'm a strong believer that experience is the best teacher, and through experience comes the most enlightening lessons. It's for this reason that I will provide some background about my own personal life. I have "walked the talk." I have found a path to happiness, but only after stumbling down many roads of destruction.

I was born and raised in Pittsburgh, Pennsylvania. My early childhood experiences were not that unusual for a child growing up during the 1940's in a middle class family. By the time I had reached high school age, I had developed all of the fears and insecurities of a typical teenager. When I graduated from high school, my parents gave me $500 so I could attend a college in Ohio that had a work/study program. During the next six years, I worked my way through undergraduate school by doing odd jobs in an automotive foundry and by cooking hamburgers in a local snackbar. It took me a long time to obtain what normally is considered a four year education, but I gained a great deal of practical experience along the way. I then attended graduate school. Although I didn't have any savings to pay for tuition, I was able to meet my expenses by working full-time as a graduate research assistant. During the next four years, I earned a Master of Science in Metallurgy and a Doctor of Philosophy.

As I look back at those 10 years of education, I now realize that I made many mistakes. Probably the biggest mistake was allowing other people to make major decisions for me regarding my future. The education I had worked so hard to obtain was not in the field of my choice. It was in a field that someone else had selected for me. I know now it was a huge mistake to follow someone else's thinking, instead of my own intuitive feelings.

While in college, I married a woman who was born in Germany near the end of World War II. She was a wonderful lady, although somewhat emotionally unstable as a result of her terrifying childhood. As a young child, she lived through the destruction of Germany and was raised by a dejected and broken-hearted mother, who was widowed during the war. Shortly after we were married, her brother, who had shared basically the same childhood experiences in Germany and who also was emotionally unstable, committed suicide. From that day on, my wife told me nearly everyday that she wanted to die. Four years later, she also committed suicide. She left behind a 2 year old son and a despondent husband.

I remember sitting alone with my son in a restaurant after the funeral wondering what I was going to do. I was aware that I needed daily help raising him, but I didn't know where I was going to get it. All my relatives were living in other states and, therefore, were unable to assist me. I didn't have many close friends, and I wasn't involved with a church. In fact, at this time of my life I had doubts about the necessity of churches and the existence of God. I believed that maybe a God did create the universe, but no longer existed. Or, if He did exist, He wasn't concerned about me. I felt very alone and totally abandoned.

Six months later, I remarried. I didn't remarry for the usual reasons. There wasn't any real love in the relationship. It was a convenience marriage. I needed a babysitter and someone to help me pick up the pieces in my life, and she wanted financial security. We both tried to make the relationship work, even though we knew there wasn't any foundation for the marriage. The marriage ended in two years.

During those two years of marriage, there were other personal problems occurring in my life. Because my mind was so severely burdened with marital problems, I was unable to perform the managerial duties at my office and, therefore, was demoted to a lower position. The company didn't reduce my pay, but I lost my large private office and all the prestigious benefits of that position. That demotion probably did more harm to me than the divorce, because I felt at that time that my work was the only stable area remaining in my life. Now as I think about those troublesome times, I realize that my life was in complete shambles. There were no stable areas.

After the second marriage ended, I became a true bachelor father. It was a wonderful experience for me, and my son and I became very close. He was my 5 year old "buddy," and we shared many memorable times together. As I look back I see that in spite of my good intentions, I made many mistakes raising my son. At this stage of my life, I was living with walls around my feelings and, because of that, I wasn't able to provide the loving, nurturing environment a young child needs. I was a bachelor father for three years.

I met my current wife in 1976, about a year after I had become a bachelor father. I honestly believe that she fell in love with my son first and then me. I used to tell her that my son and I were a "package deal;" if she wanted my son, she must also take me. We married after two years of dating for the right reason, we were in love.

During the early part of this marriage, my wife became aware of the walls that were surrounding my emotions. She noticed I had great difficulty dropping my shields and letting my true feelings show. I hardly ever got angry, and I hardly ever laughed. I was like an emotionless computer with a lot of stored information. All my decisions were very logical.

In 1984, I became involved with a church. This greatly surprised most of my friends, because they thought I was an atheist. Actually, I was never an atheist, but was an agnostic for 25 years. There is a significant difference between the two. An atheist rejects all religious beliefs and denies the existence of God, whereas an agnostic questions the existence of God in the absence of material proof. At this time in my life, I just wasn't aware of any information that accurately confirmed that there was, or wasn't, a God.

My involvement with the church wasn't because of a conscious desire for spiritual enlightenment, although the church was very spiritual. I started to attend the Church of Today in the Detroit area for only one reason, because it provided the best motivational talks in the city. The guest speakers at the church were always discussing such things as how to develop a positive attitude, how to increase self-esteem, and ways to achieve major goals. One talented speaker in particular, Mike Wickett, was so inspiring that, after listening to him, I decided to quit my engineering position at General Motors and start my own consulting company. I remember Mike saying,

"If your life is a struggle, you're probably on the wrong path." After thinking about what he had said, I finally realized my life was a major struggle, and I wasn't doing the things that made me happy.

After going to the Church of Today for about a year, I attended a three-day men's spiritual retreat that was sponsored by the church. It changed my life. The leaders of the retreat had divided the group of 200 men into smaller groups of eight. Each of the small groups were given a set of questions to discuss at their table. The first question was, "What event in your life has caused you the most pain?" I decided to get honest with myself for a change, and got in touch with the event. I began to cry. Crying was new to me. I hadn't cried for over 14 years.

As I sat there with tears running down my cheeks, the minister, Jack Boland, came to our table and asked me what event was causing me so much pain. I told him it was the suicide of my first wife, and I couldn't forgive her for leaving me the way she did, and I couldn't forgive myself for not helping her more with her illness. Jack Boland took my hand, and said softly to me, "Think about the event. Did your wife do the best she could under the circumstances?" I thought for a while, and then said, "Yes." Jack said, "Accept the fact that she did the best she could, and release her by forgiving her." And I did. It was that easy, and it happened that quickly. Then Jack said to me, "Did you do the best you could at that particular time in your life in helping her with her illness?" I thought for a few minutes, and answered, "Yes, I did." Jack said, "Then release yourself from the pain by forgiving yourself." This was much more difficult for me than forgiving her, but I finally forgave myself on a conscious level. During those ten minutes of being in touch with my innermost feelings, I had taken the first step towards true forgiveness. I had developed a mental attitude that would allow lasting forgiveness, a spiritual healing, to occur. I was now starting to release 14 years of deep-seated anger and pain.

When I arrived home from that weekend retreat, I knew I was a different person. It wasn't just obvious to me, but my wife and son also noticed the difference. They were now seeing a softer side of me. A side I had protected with mental walls for a long time.

Three months later, my deceased wife of 14 years visited me. I was lying in bed one evening thinking about the day's activities. It was a hot summer night, and I remember the curtains blowing in the window. As I lay there on my back, staring at the ceiling, she appeared at the foot of the bed. I could only see her from the waist up. She looked just as I remembered her, except her hair was longer. It was the length when we first met. We talked, but not with words. Somehow we communicated through our minds. She said, "Hello, David. Are you at peace?" And I said, "Yes." She said, "That's good. I just wanted to tell you that you're doing a great job raising our son." I said, "Thank you." Then she left. I lay there for about an hour thinking about the experience before I fell asleep. The experience was very peaceful and assuring. It was from this occurrence that I became aware that life is eternal, that there is no such thing as death.

After that experience, I had a burning desire to learn more about spirituality. I used to think, is it possible there is a spiritual world interwoven with the natural world? Is it possible that we can use our minds through prayer and meditation to create joyful situations? Is it possible that the unbelievable statements and promises in the Bible are actually true? I had to investigate.

I started my investigation by reading books on religious beliefs and practices. From this I became very interested in meditation. Not the kind of meditation that is practiced in many Eastern religions, but a simpler type, a Christian type. To prepare for meditation, I would lay face-up on the floor, close my eyes, and listen to tranquilizing sounds of nature that were pre-recorded on special cassette tapes. While in the meditative state, I would think about the deeper meaning of life. I would think about who I was, and why I was living on Earth. I would think about God, and if He really existed, why I couldn't experience Him directly. Each daily meditation would last about an hour. The meditations were extremely peaceful.

After meditating daily for about six months, a strange thing occurred. A bright light started to appear in my meditations while my eyes were closed. It wasn't a blinding light, but it was very bright. At first, I would open my eyes to see if something had changed in the room that would have caused the brightness to occur, but there were never any changes. After a few weeks of experiencing the light, I realized the light was trying to communicate with me. If an answer to a question asked in meditation was "yes," the intensity of the light increased. If an answer to a question asked in meditation was "no," the light decreased in brightness.

At first, I didn't know what the light represented. Was it my subconscious mind, or was it Spirit? So I started to ask questions in meditation that would give me some clues as to the identity of the light. If the light could provide me with some insights about future events, then I would acknowledge the light as Spirit, since only Spirit knows what will occur in the future. If the light could only answer questions about the past or present, then I would conclude that the light was just my subconscious mind communicating with me. After a few days of experimenting, it became clear to me that the light, without a doubt, was Spirit.

A few months later, I read the book, *Man's Eternal Quest,* by the great spiritual leader, Paramahansa Yogananda. In this book, the presence of the light in meditation is discussed. Yogananda, who was considered an expert on spiritual meditation, refers to the bright light that appears in deep meditation as the "Light of God." It's that part of God, our Christ Consciousness, the Holy Spirit, that is within each of us. The Bible also informs us that "God is Light" (1 John 1:5), and that the Holy Spirit lives within us (1 Corinthians 6:19). Based on all of my spiritual readings, I now believe that the Holy Spirit is the bright light that appears in my meditations.

Being able to communicate one-on-one with the Holy Spirit in meditation is my greatest joy today. These spiritual meditations have provided me with a great deal of information about life. In fact, most of the spiritual knowledge that is in this book has come from this source. I have learned from my discussions with the Light, that everyone of us on Earth has the same ability to communicate with Spirit. It makes no difference what we have done in the past. The clarity of our communications depends only on our current spiritual beliefs and our willingness to surrender our wills to God. In Part Three of this program, we will discuss how to communicate directly with God through a Christian meditation.

The Light in my daily meditation is my guiding light. Every major decision I have made during the past few years, whether rational or irrational, has been based on directions I have received from the Light. Each morning, I go into meditation and ask for my daily assignments. Sometimes I'm told to write letters to certain influential people, to call and support troubled acquaintances, to follow-up on certain business deals, or to just enjoy the beautiful day. Sometimes I see the direct benefits of my actions, and sometimes I don't. One thing is for sure, however, I always follow the directions I receive from the Light. I have total trust that Spirit knows what is best for me.

 My current spiritual beliefs are relatively simple. I believe we are all part of a pure loving Spirit, incarnated as human beings, living on Earth to correct minor imperfections in our souls. I believe we all have unlimited spiritual powers. I no longer believe in the limitations that we, as humans, have placed on ourselves. I believe Jesus was trying to tell us that we have unlimited powers, when he said, "In solemn truth I tell you, anyone believing in me shall do the same miracles I have done, and even greater ones." (John 14:12)

Becoming a deeply spiritual person hasn't put any restrictions on my life, but has set me free to enjoy what life on Earth has to offer. It has set me free from the most common fears and worries. It has set me free from loneliness. It has filled my life with an abundance, both material and nonmaterial, that I never believed possible. It has helped me to appreciate what I have and to believe that whatever I need will be provided for me. It has helped me to forgive and to accept everyone as an equal, no matter what act they have committed. It has also allowed me to see that we are all individualized expressions of the same loving God.

It has been five years since my deceased wife visited me, and four years since I started meditating. During these past few years, dozens of spiritual events have occurred in my life. Some are very personal, and some are unbelievable. If the purpose of this transformation program was to document spiritual events, I would probably just list several of these occurrences right now. But the purpose of this program is to help you understand yourself and to learn how to apply spiritual principles in your daily life. I believe if this objective is satisfied, each of you will have your own spiritual experiences to treasure. There is definitely a spiritual world interwoven with our natural world. Are you ready to discover it?

There is definitely a spiritual world interwoven with our natural world. Are you ready to discover it?

FOLLOW-UP EXERCISES

(1) Write a full description of the person you would like to become. Describe the mental, physical, and spiritual qualities of this person. Describe the relationships you want to have with significant people in your life. Get in touch with the feelings you would have if you were to become this ideal person.

(2) Now act as if you were the person you described above. By believing you are this ideal person, you will quickly become this person. The spiritual Law of Belief, which will be discussed in a later chapter, will help you in becoming the person you desire to be.

—PART ONE—

Spiritual Knowledge

"Spiritual Knowledge is the key to human happiness"

—Day #2—

Discovering who you __really__ are

About three years ago, I was sitting in my office at General Motors thinking, "I don't belong here anymore." It wasn't that I was unhappy, or that General Motors wasn't good to me, because the company did treat me very fairly. It was just that it was time to move on, to do my own thing, to take control of my life. So I planned a career change. I was well aware of the fact that I didn't have the required financial support to make a major change, so I asked God for some help. I said, "God, please send me about fifteen thousand dollars, so I can start my own business." A few weeks later, I received an unexpected check for $15,000 from the estate of a distant relative who had died a few years earlier. I had no idea I would be receiving money from that estate.

Having underestimated how much money I would need to start the new business, I went back to God a month later and asked for some additional money. This time I wasn't going to leave myself short of cash, so I asked God for $100,000 to cover the total start-up cost of the business. Three weeks later, I was given some wonderful news. I was told that General Motors management had reversed its decision, and that the company was going to give me a separation check when I left. Originally, I had been told that if I quit the company, I wouldn't get any separation benefits. The check was for $101,543. I now had all the money I needed to start my new consulting business.

With the initial financial problems resolved, it was time to face another major problem. How was I going to let executives of small manufacturing companies know that I was available as a technical marketing consultant. I had never been a consultant before, so how was I going to find an executive to hire me? Not knowing how to resolve this issue, I said another prayer to God. I said, "God, I need your help again. I need clients for my business, but I don't know how to inform executives that I'm available for hire as a consultant." The next day in meditation I was told not to worry about the problem and that it would be resolved shortly. A week later, a writer for the Wall Street Journal approached me and asked if he could include me in an article he was writing. I agreed, and two months later, on May 26, 1987, there was a front page article in the Wall Street Journal that reported that I was leaving a secure position at General Motors to start my own business. The article told the readers the exact service I was offering and gave the address of my new company. I'm sure that thousands of business executives read that front page article. One week after the article appeared in the paper, I signed my first consulting contract. It was with an executive who had read the article. The contract was only for 60 days, but it paid me more money than what I was earning at General Motors in one year. After that first contract, I was booked months in advance for additional consulting services.

By this time, I was well aware that a powerful Source was filling my life with miracles. It was clear to me that it wasn't because of my own efforts that my business was doing so well. In fact, I really wasn't putting that much effort into the business. But it seemed as if everything I asked for, I got. Realizing that God was the source of my good fortune, I made a deal with Him, if that is possible. I said, "God, I will turn my life over to you and will do everything you ask of me, if you will teach me how to be happy." The deal was made. We agreed that I would live day-to-day and would never know what exciting events were around the corner. This has been very difficult for me, since by nature I'm a planner. But it has all worked out splendidly. My life has truly been blessed since I have learned to "let go and let God." Because of my faith and trust in the spiritual system, I now have everything in life I could ever want. My life is filled with love and prosperity.

As I look back at the past decade, I realize that my increase in happiness during the last three years is a direct result of a new understanding of who I really am. It's the awareness of my spiritual powers that has set me free to enjoy life to its fullest. These spiritual powers are not unique to me. You also have them. And this is what I would like to talk about during the next two lessons. Are you ready to learn who you really are and how to take advantage of God's Spiritual Laws? If so, you'll greatly benefit from the next two lessons.

Searching for deeper answers

Many of us are so busy with our daily activities, that we don't take the time to think about the basic questions concerning life, such as who we really are and why we are living on Earth. Normally when these types of questions are asked, simple answers are found. And often, these simple answers are adequate. But when these types of questions are asked, we really should search deeper for answers. Sometimes by probing, a totally new understanding is discovered. This is particularly true when the questions involve spirituality.

As an illustration of searching deeper to find a more truthful answer to a simple question, let's consider the following.

Question: When did my son's life begin?
Answer: He was born on August 7, 1970.

This is a good answer and probably acceptable to most people, but it's not the most truthful answer. Some of you are probably thinking you know a better answer. It was the day he was conceived. And this is a better answer, so we'll back the date nine months to November 7, 1969. I'm sure if we stopped here, many of you would go away thinking you knew the correct answer. But there is an earlier date. The sperm and the egg from which my son developed were being formed much earlier. But there was still an earlier date. Five years earlier, my first wife and I agreed to have a child, and we dreamed of having a son. So my son's life actually began in our minds as a beautiful idea five years before he was conceived. Yet, there was even an earlier date. When I was a young boy, I told my parents that when I grew up, I wanted to have a son. So my son's life actually began in my mind as an idea 20 years earlier. Is there still an earlier date? I think so. Somewhere in time,

God decided in His mind that my son would be born, and His decision may have occurred many years earlier.

The point of this illustration is that many of us believe we know all of the right answers to simple questions, but we don't. Unless we are willing to search deeper for answers, we really won't discover the true meaning of life. The greatest truths about your life are available to you right now. But to find them, you must be willing to go within and listen to your Higher Power. Your Higher Power is that part of God that lives within you. It's that part of God that is often referred to as your soul, your Christ Consciousness, or the Holy Spirit. The best way to listen to your Higher Power is through a peaceful meditation.

The greatest truths about your life will come from within, from meditation, from listening to your Higher Power.

Understanding who you really are

The most important question you'll ever ask yourself is, "Who am I?" When you know the truest answer to that question, the second most important question will be asked automatically. And that question is, "How can I serve God?"

So let's answer the first question: Who are you?
The answer is: No one knows who you are, except you.

Your Higher Power knows exactly who you are and why you are living on Earth. The Higher Power that exists within you knows all your thoughts, all your feelings, all your fears, as well as every other aspect of your life. More importantly, your Higher Power knows how you can live a life on this Earth that is filled with love and happiness. Your Higher Power knows of the life that a loving

God has created for you. To find out who you are, all you have to do is contact your Higher Power and ask the question. Unfortunately, most of us are unable to meditate deeply enough to do this. So let me tell you who I am based on conversations with my Higher Power, and maybe from this description you'll discover who you really are.

Because I'm a "visual person," it's easier for me to describe myself by using a simple visual model. In this model, we'll assume that I consist of two components. The first part is called the Human Being component, and the second part is called the Spiritual Being component. When these two components are brought together, they form a human/spiritual living structure called the Total Being. This complex Total Being is me. It's what people experience with their senses when they interact with me. This model is illustrated on the next page.

My Human Being component consists of my human body and my ego. This is the part of me that is "flesh and blood." This is the part of me that grew from a baby into an adult and will someday die and be buried. My Human Being component is that part of my Total Being that evolved many millions of years ago from the lower animal kingdom. The evolution of my Human Being component is described in Charles Darwin's famous Theory of Evolution. My Human Being component is just a vehicle for travel, a form of transportation on this Earth for my Spiritual Being component. My Human Being component has little importance in God's overall plan for spiritual unity. It's that part of me that the Bible says will return to dust long after I die. My Human Being component is currently 185 pounds of "clay."

The Spiritual Being component is my soul. It's the God Spirit within me that contains my Higher Power, as well as many other supernatural powers. It's the part of me that will never die, but has eternal life. My Spiritual Being component evolved from God at the beginning of time, and has always been, and will always be, a part of God. It's the spirit within me that connects me to every other living thing in this abundantly alive universe. It's the part of me that is referred to in the Bible when it states, "God created man in His image and likeness."

The Two Components of Your "TOTAL BEING"

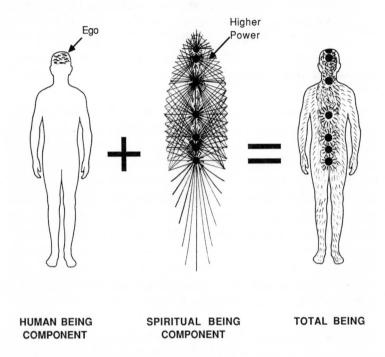

Ego

Higher Power

| HUMAN BEING | SPIRITUAL BEING | TOTAL BEING |
| COMPONENT | COMPONENT | |

The "image and likeness" of God isn't the human form as many of us have been taught, but is the Spiritual Being part of us. Our Spiritual Being component is a loving, invisible spirit that has unlimited powers. This mighty spirit is within each of us, and to activate its unlimited powers, all we have to do is believe. Jesus was telling us the importance of believing in the unlimited powers of the Spiritual Being when he said, "All things are possible to him that believes."

*All things are possible to him
that believes.*

Mark 9:23

You are more than human

Most of us don't accept the idea that we have unlimited powers. In fact, many of us believe that our personal powers are limited by the capabilities of our physical bodies and by the intellectual capacities of our minds. Many of us believe that we are limited by the restrictions of our Human Being components and are unwilling to acknowledge the powers that can flow through our Spiritual Beings. Those who believe they have limitations in power will probably live their lives filled with limitations. On the other hand, those who believe they have super-human powers will experience these powers if their beliefs are strong. I believe that Jesus was telling us that we are "more than human" and have an amazing ability to perform miracles, when he said:

**Truly, truly, I say to you, he who believes in me, the works that I do, shall he do also; and greater works than these shall he do.
(John 14:12)**

Does this passage from the Bible mean that we have the ability to walk on water and to heal the human body as Jesus did? Does this passage mean that we can even perform greater miracles than He did? Yes. Absolutely, yes. That's what Jesus was telling us. You can perform miracles, if your belief system is strong enough. You can do anything you truly believe you can do. The prerequisite is that you must believe it at a deep spiritual level and not just at a superficial intellectual level. I understand that this sounds incredible, but I also know that, "With God all things are possible."

In all my readings of spiritual books, I have never found

anything that suggested that man is limited by his human capabilities. Most of the religious books I have read, including the Bible, state that man is only limited by his thoughts, by what he believes he can do. Most of the people in this world, however, are still living by the old saying, "When I see it, I'll believe it." Ironically, the reverse statement is more often true. "When you believe it, you'll see it."

Does God answer all our prayers?

We can communicate directly with God any time of the day we desire through our Spiritual Being components. There are no special arrangements that must be made. We don't need another person with us. We don't need to be in a church or religious place of worship. We don't need a history of devotion to God. In fact, we don't even need a strong belief that there is a God. All we need to have at a particular moment is an open heart and an honest, sincere desire to communicate with Him. The best way to communicate with God is through prayer and meditation.

I'm sure some people believe that God doesn't hear all our prayers, or if He does, He only answers a small percentage of them. The truth is, because of His loving concern for us, God answers all our prayers, but the answers aren't always what we expect or want. The answers are, however, the best answers for the spiritual enlightenment of our souls.

Based on my meditations, there are three situations in which our prayers **are not** answered by God in the manner we request. They are the following:

(1) *When a prayer results in a decrease in harmony and love on a universal level.* A prayer that would bring harm to another person would not be honored by God, since Divine Love is the driving energy behind all prayer responses.

(2) *When the fulfillment of a prayer is in direct conflict with the spiritual path of an individual.* An example would be if God wanted a person to change her career and become a minister. In this situation, God may answer certain prayers concerning her current career in such a way that it would result in the women wanting to leave her particular job and seek a more fulfilling position as a

spiritual leader. This is a very important concept to understand, because if you're having major difficulties in your life, it's probably because you're drifting away from your spiritual path. Life was created to be a happy, exciting experience in which we learn certain spiritual truths. Difficulty only comes when we're resisting the spiritual truths we're suppose to learn. And the more we resist, the greater the difficulty.

(3) *When God has a better idea.* Because God knows everything, He's in a position to help us create happier lives by assisting us in our daily activities. When you don't get something you pray for, give thanks to God for denying your prayer request. Just assume that He has used His greater knowledge of the overall situation in making His decision, and then believe that you'll get something even better. This belief that something better will happen is required to make it happen.

An example of believing the best will occur is a situation that happened last year when my wife, Gail, and I were trying to buy a house on a particular lake. We had discussed the general details of the house we wanted to buy for about two months. We wanted a relatively new, medium size house of a modern design on a certain lake about 30 miles north of Detroit. Being a visual person who believes we can create situations and objects with our minds, I drew several pictures in a tablet of the ideal house. I drew the floor plans, the lot layout, and the general location on the lake. About a month later, a house came up for sale on that very lake. It wasn't exactly what we wanted, but we did submit an offer to purchase it. We prayed for a week that the offer would be accepted, and because most of our prayers are answered, we just assumed the sale would go through. To our surprise, in the middle of the negotiations, another family approached the sellers and offered more money than we were willing to spend. So our bid to purchase the house was rejected.

Believing that something better would happen, we waited. A few months later, a friend called my wife, and told her there was another house for sale on the premium side of that lake. The following Sunday we went out and looked at the house. The house had the exact floor plan that was on my drawing of the ideal house. All the rooms were located exactly in the right place and were of the proper size. The lot and location were very similar to my drawings, and even nicer than we had pictured. The house cost even less than the house we had previously considered. So we made a bid to buy that house on Monday. The sellers countered our offer on Tuesday, and we bought the house on Wednesday. There was no doubt in my mind that God wanted us to have this particular house. God's desire for us to make this move was again confirmed the following week, when we listed our old house on a Wednesday afternoon, and by that Friday, we had an official purchase offer from the buyers. The importance of maintaining faith can't be overstated. One of the main reasons we are living right now in our ideal house is because we had faith in God's love and greater wisdom.

Your spiritual powers are unlimited if your faith is strong.

FOLLOW-UP EXERCISES

(1) Think about situations in your life that suggest that you are "more than human." Have you experienced any miracles in your life lately or been involved in any events that were supernatural? Think about it.

(2) Find a quiet place that is free from all distracting noise. Get comfortable, close your eyes, and let your mind recall the most peaceful place you have ever been. When you are feeling totally relaxed, ask yourself who you really are. Listen for the answer with your heart. (You may want to listen to a special meditation tape while you are relaxing. Many people have better results meditating when they have soft music playing in the background.)

—Day #3—

Understanding Spiritual Laws

Recently I heard a wise old philosopher say:

**Man's happiness is controlled by a hundred
laws and influenced by a million rules,
but only the laws are important.**

When I first heard this statement, I wasn't sure what he meant by
it. But as I listened to the old man talk, I realized he was right, that
our happiness is determined by our willingness to obey certain
spiritual laws. By living within these spiritual laws on a daily basis,
our lives are blessed with love and prosperity. Are you interested
in learning about the spiritual laws that can bring you happiness?
We are going to discuss a few of them in this lesson.

The reason I originally found the old philosopher's statement
difficult to understand was because I thought a rule and a law were
basically the same. But there is a difference, and for our discussion
it's important that we establish separate meanings. In this lesson
we will use the following dictionary definitions:

RULE — an established guideline for action or conduct.
— a fixed standard for determining habits or customs.
— a complete set of regulations in a religious order.

LAW — a sequence of events in nature or in human activities
that has been observed to occur with unvarying
uniformity under the same conditions.

— the controlling principles in God's universe.
— God's Natural Laws.

Based on the above definitions, a rule is just a guide for living. It's a suggested or accepted way of doing things. It doesn't absolutely dictate what will happen if one does or doesn't follow a suggested guideline. A rule is exorable, it can be influenced by pleas. A rule is mutable, it can be changed. A rule is revocable, it can be withdrawn or cancelled. The so-called "laws" that man has created to control society are not laws, but are actually just rules. All of them are exorable, mutable, and revocable. Our societal "laws" also don't state precisely what the consequences will be for a person who breaks a rule. For an example, a person who kills another human being may or may not be punished for the crime. In certain situations, such as in war, taking another person's life is acceptable, even though one of God's rules says, "Thou shalt not kill."

In the Bible, we are given many rules to live by. The Ten Commandments are not laws, but are actually rules. They are a set of rules for living a life based on God's Will. By breaking these rules, and I have broken my share, it doesn't mean that when we die we'll be punished for eternity. Rules don't establish the final outcome of a situation. When we break a Commandment, it only means that we're not living our lives at that particular moment in the manner God desires us to.

A law by definition states exactly what the outcome for a particular situation will be, based on the individual actions that occur during the event. True laws are not flexible. In fact, they are inexorable, immutable, and irrevocable. God's Natural Laws, both the Physical and Spiritual Laws, are the only true laws that exist. Most scientists agree that the Natural Laws have been around since the creation of the universe, over 15 billion years ago. God's spiritual laws are the "laws" the old philosopher was referring to in the earlier statement when he said that laws control our happiness. These are the laws that we must understand to create happier lives.

God's Natural Laws

When God created the universe, He created two groups of natural laws. The first group of laws was established to bring order to the physical universe, while the second group of laws was designed to help man advance on his spiritual path. It has only been during the past 500 years that our scientists, with a working knowledge of physical laws, have been able to accurately predict physical occurrences in the universe. Because of our understanding of God's physical law of gravitation, we can now calculate for any date in the future, the precise location of many planets and stars. It's because of our understanding of God's physical laws of physics and chemistry that we have been able to land a man on the moon and send a satellite into deep space. It's also because of our understanding of God's physical laws of electricity and fluid mechanics that we have highly sophisticated medical equipment for transplanting hearts and kidneys. Our knowledge of God's physical laws has helped us to discover and explore our physical environment.

God's spiritual laws, which have been created to help man complete his spiritual journey, are not as well known or understood as God's physical laws. This isn't surprising since the spiritual laws are based on intuitive feelings and faith, whereas the physical laws are based on intellectual thoughts and logic. In today's society, logic is considered more acceptable as a foundation for laws than intuition. God's spiritual laws, however, are just as accurate and predictable as His physical laws and can be used to greatly enhance our daily lives.

True happiness comes from understanding, and living within, God's spiritual laws. It's from this understanding that many of us will be able to create the quality of life we eagerly seek.

True happiness comes from understanding, and living within, God's spiritual laws.

Law of Cause and Effect

The Law of Cause and Effect, which was created by God for our spiritual development, is considered by many to be the most important spiritual law. This law has been described in many spiritual books throughout the centuries, including the Bible. Although it has been stated in many ways, its significance hasn't been altered. The law has been stated as follows:

- **For every action in life, there is an equivalant reaction.**

- **We cause everything that happens to us. There are no accidents.**

- **Whatsoever a man soweth, that shall he also reap.**
  (Galatians 6:7)

Although this is a simple law, it really has a major effect on our daily activities. This law says that everything that occurs in our daily lives, whether or not we want it to happen, is a direct result of our previous actions. This means the actions we send out are returned back to us in a similar manner. According to this law, if we're cruel to someone, cruelty will be returned in the same amount by that person or someone else. On the other hand, if we cause someone to be happy, that person or something else is going to make us happy by an equivalent amount. Since this law never fails, this means we're 100% accountable for our daily actions. Based on this law, we never really get away with anything in life.

This law also implies that if you want "something" in life, all you have to do is send that "something" out to others. If you want casual friends, just be a casual friend. If you want loving relationships, just be loving towards others. If you want repectful children, just treat your children with respect. If you want an honest day's pay, just do an honest day's work. And if you want friendly neighbors, just be a friendly neighbor. It's that simple, and it always works.

If you want loving relationships, just be loving towards others.

Our rewards in life are also directly proportional to the amount of time and effort we dedicate towards our goals. The Bible has several passages that state this fact. Two of them are:

Every man shall receive his own reward
according to his own labor.
1 Corinthians 3:8

He which soweth sparingly shall reap also sparingly;
and he which soweth bountifully shall reap bountifully.
2 Corinthians 9:6

You can use the Law of Cause and Effect to become a more spiritual person, if you have such a desire. In order to do this, however, you must do two things. The first is to direct less time and effort towards satisfying your own personal needs and material goals, and the second is to direct more time and effort towards a spiritual development program. The amount of sincere effort you put towards a spiritual program will determine how fast, and to what degree, your spiritual growth will occur.

Spiritual Law of Thought

Probably the second most important spiritual law to understand and live by is the Law of Thought. This law states:

What you think--is what you are.

The law says that you are exactly what you think you are. If you think you're a wise and energetic person, you'll be wise and energetic in your actions. If you think you lack the ability to achieve a particular goal, you'll never achieve that goal, because you won't put forth the proper energy to accomplish it. If you think you're old and decrepit, you are. On the other hand, if you think you're young and beautiful, you are. You are exactly what you think you are!

This law has been known for thousands of years and has been stated in many ways. The Bible, in Proverbs 23:7, says:

As he thinketh in his heart, so is he.

Ralph Waldo Emerson, the great American poet and philosopher, stated the law as follows:

Man is what he thinks.

This law says whatever you are constantly thinking about, you are or quickly become. The situations in your current life are the direct result of thoughts you have been thinking up to this moment. If you're unhappy in a relationship or at your place of employment, it's probably because of your negative thoughts. If you're unable to remove yourself from these situations, it's probably because your thoughts are filled with fear and insecurity.

If you want to become a happier person, just think happier thoughts. Think about the many wonderful things that are happening to you right now. Think about the loving relationships in your life. Think about the hobbies you enjoy. Think about the health problems you don't have, instead of those that you do. Be appreciative of what you have, and accepting of what hasn't yet come your way. Think about the fact that you're totally protected at all times by a loving God. If you think happy thoughts, you'll be a happy person.

The Law of Thought is the principle behind all the "positive thinking" and "creative imaging" books that are being sold today. The law guarantees that if you think positively, you'll be positive and will experience positive situations. On the other hand, the law also guarantees that if you think negatively, you'll be negative and will experience negative situations.

The law also implies that you can create your physical environment with your thoughts. For example, if you have a desire to live in the city of New York, constantly think about living there and being a New Yorker, and soon you'll attract all the right circumstances and find yourself moving there. Through creative imaging you can use your mind to create whatever you want. The Law of Thought is a fascinating law that opens the door to unlimited possibilities. When my wife and I found our perfect dream house on the lake (see earlier lesson), it was because we had first created mental pictures of the ideal house in our minds. Those pictures were later put on paper, but it was the energy of our thoughts that brought us and the house together. Because of our creative imaging, we attracted the perfect house.

You can have everything you want in life, if you can control your thoughts. Gautama Buddha, the founder of Buddhism, understood this law when he said, "All that we are is the result of what we have thought."

All that we are is the result of what we have thought.

Buddha

Spiritual Law of Belief

The Law of Belief is basically the same as the Law of Thought. It says that whatever you believe in your heart comes true. Throughout the Bible we're told how important it is to believe in God, in ourselves, and in our prayers. In Mark 9:11, we are told:

All things are possible to him that believes.

One of my favorite rules for living is based on both the Law of Thought and the Law of Belief. This rule says:

If my mind can conceive it,
and my heart can believe it,
better start preparing for it,
because I'm going to see it.

This is an important rule for me, because it provides me with some insight into future projects and gives me time to prepare for them. The writing of this book is a good example. When I first thought about writing this book, I didn't believe I could do it. I have a reading disorder, and because of that, I have great difficulty reading books. Although I have struggled through many technical and medical books, I have never been able to read more than a few pages of a novel. Reading is just too laborious for me. Writing is even more painful. This book never got off the ground until I started to believe that my Higher Power would help me write it. Once I truly believed I could write this book, I went into action and prepared for the endeavor by setting up a special office and organizing writing materials. The chapters then started to materialize one-by-one. Believing is one of the first steps to seeing.

Spiritual Law of Abundance

The spiritual Law of Abundance says there is an unlimited supply of "everything" you'll ever need while living in God's universe. According to this law, there isn't just an overabundance of such things as love, support, faith, and happiness, but there is also an overabundance of material goods, food, and money. If you're not receiving an adequate quantity of any of these necessities for life, it may be because you're resisting the natural flow of these gifts to you. Because these gifts are so plentiful, we should all be willing to give them away to others. It will be through the "giving" that our lives will be abundantly blessed.

Spiritual Law of Perfection

The Law of Perfection says that everything in the universe is "perfect" just the way it is. Many of us have difficulty believing this law, because we're aware of the many vicious acts that take place daily in our society. It's difficult to think that the rapes and murders that occur are part of "God's Perfection." The truth is, it is God's perfection in action. In order to understand this, however, we must be able to accept the idea that God would allow the most devastating events to occur on Earth so our souls can learn the lessons they need to learn. Our souls, as well as our physical minds, learn the most difficult lessons when they are exposed to the severest situations. Sometimes, we must experience mental and physical pain before we're able to understand.

Spiritual Law of Tenfold Return

The Law of Tenfold Return is a very interesting law that many of us have heard about in church, but have not taken advantage of. This law, which is also know as the Law of Tithing, is related to the Law of Cause and Effect and to the Law of Abundance. The law states that whatever you give to the service of God will be returned to you tenfold. This means if you give $100 to a church, you'll receive ten times that amount of money ($1,000) back from a "source". The immediate pay-back source isn't defined by the law. The money that is returned to you may come back in cash, as a check, or in the form of a job in which you're able to earn an additional $1,000. Or it may come back in some other way, but it will come back as a tenfold return. There is one stipulation to this law. In order to receive the tenfold return, the donor must believe that the tenfold formula will work. The law does not work if you don't believe in it.

In the Bible, in Malachi 3:10, God said:

**Bring all the tithes [10% of all your earnings]
into the storehouse so that there will be
food enough in my Temple; if you do,
I will open up the windows of heaven for you
and pour out a blessing so great you won't
have room enough to take it in!**

I personally have found that this law works very well. In fact, during a recent three month period, I received over $115,000 from two sources as a result of pledging $11,500 to a church. The money that I received to start my new consulting business (see earlier lesson) came to me as a result of tithing. I gave a church $1,500 a few weeks before I asked God for $15,000 for my business. And when I needed the $100,000 for my business, I told God in meditation and wrote in my daily journal, that I would give 10% of the money to a church if I received the money. A few days after I received the check for $101,000, I gave my church a check for $10,100. It's only by giving that we can receive, and the more we give, the more we'll receive.

Others Spiritual Laws

There are several other spiritual laws that are worth knowing. Most of them, however, are related to the ones we already addressed. If you have a desire to learn more about the spiritual laws of the universe, I suggest you obtain a copy of *The Supreme Philosophy of Man* by Alfred Montapert. This book describes 47 universal laws.

God's laws are perfect. They protect us, make us wise, and give us joy and light. God's laws are pure, eternal, just. They are more desirable than gold. For they warn us away from harm and give success to those who obey them.

Psalm 19: 7-11

FOLLOW-UP EXERCISES

(1) The Law of Cause and Effect is a powerful law that always works. Which situations in your life have you "caused"? Which situations would you like to change? You have the power to improve your life.

(2) You are exactly where you are in life because of what you have been thinking and believing. What have you been thinking about lately? What do you truly believe? Is it time to let go of old beliefs?

—Day #4—

Finding your real purpose in life

Most of us, at one time or another, have thought about the following questions: Why am I alive? What is the real purpose of my life? Why do I have the parents I do? Why was my childhood so difficult? Is there more to my life than what I'm conscious of? Why am I experiencing so much pain in my current relationships? Why did my friend die prematurely? Is death the final chapter of life?

These are all very important questions, and many of us have spent countless hours discussing them. Some of us have found these questions to be very frustrating, because our intellectual minds, our logical thought process, can't answer them. But the answers to these questions are known by you. They are known by your Higher Power, your God within. And they can be learned through meditation.

Unfortunately, most of us don't meditate deeply enough to be able to learn the answers. So let me tell you a fictitious story that is filled with many truths about life, and you be the judge about what is true and what isn't. Let your intuition be your guide. Before you read this story, however, I would like you to completely relax in a quiet location that is free of all distractions. When you are settled, you may want to say a short prayer and ask the God within, the Holy Spirit, to assist you in understanding the truth about life. It's only the spiritual side of you that can fully acknowledge the depth of this story. The path to spiritual knowledge is paved with quiet minds and open hearts.

*The path to spiritual knowledge is
paved with quiet minds
and open hearts.*

Story of Angel Marcus

Once upon a time in a far away place on the other side of the universe near the star of Kutume, a group of God's perfect angels were playing. The angels were very happy and shared a special love, as they floated effortlessly among the planets and stars. They were in a state of total peacefulness, because they knew they were a special part of the "oneness" of God.

One of the angels, known as Marcus, was not quite as contented as the others, because of a minor imperfection in his otherwise perfect angelic form. Marcus' imperfection was his inability to forgive instantaneously. He had been aware of this condition for several years and decided it was time to correct it. He told the other angels about his minor flaw and requested their support in correcting it. All the angels agreed to help their loving friend.

It was decided that the best thing Marcus could do to correct his minor imperfection would be to visit one of the planets in the universe that God had created solely for the correction of spiritual deficiencies. Although angel Marcus had his choice of many planets to visit, he decided to visit the planet called Earth, because Earth had the best programs for correcting imperfections. Marcus understood that on Earth, he would inhabit a human body and be exposed to severe situations in which he would experience the full range of emotions. He realized it would be through these difficult experiences that he would learn the most significant lessons and that the lessons were necessary in order to correct his minor imperfection. So he started designing the perfect plan for his lifetime visit to Earth.

Since Marcus' imperfection was his inability to instantaneously forgive, many situations had to be designed into his Earth visit that would provide opportunities to experience unforgiveness, as well as forgiveness. Marcus realized that the perfect plan must allow all feelings associated with forgiveness to be experienced, if the imperfection in his angelic soul was to be corrected. As Marcus worked on his plan, several of the other angels offered suggestions and agreed to be involved in the visit to Earth. One of Marcus' closest angelic friends, named Angela, lovingly agreed to be a participant in a major event on Earth that would provide Marcus with an opportunity to experience forgiveness. Angela had agreed to return home early from her visit to Earth by ending the life of the human body she would inhabit. Her premature death would occur in a car accident.

Once the general plan was sketched out, it was time to fill in the details. Marcus had many basic decisions to make for his lifetime trip including such things as which sex to be, which country to live in, which parents to have, and which types of childhood events would be helpful. It was important that each of these decisions be made correctly, since they would all greatly affect the type of personality and belief system Marcus would develop on Earth. Marcus knew that his Earthly personality and belief system would influence how well he would learn his spiritual lessons. After weeks of planning, the final plan, the Divine Plan, was completed. All that was needed now was approval by one of the head spiritual leaders.

So Marcus met with Jesus to get His approval for the plan. Jesus, who was the head spiritual leader, had taken a great interest in the spiritual programs on planet Earth. He was considered by many to be the most knowledgeable Spirit concerning "Earth University" as He affectionately referred to the planet. Jesus approved Marcus' plan for visiting Earth and went over the rules for the visit. The rules were few and simple. Once born on Earth as a human, Marcus would automatically forget on a conscious level all about his true identity as an angel, and would live on Earth as a human being until his Divine Plan was completed. His Divine Plan didn't include every event that would occur in his Earth visit, but it did include all of the significant events. Upon completion of the plan and the death of the human body, all remembrance of the true self, the God Spirit, would return to him.

As the meeting was concluding, Jesus told Marcus a few final things. Jesus said, "Many times during your visit on Earth you're going to feel lost and confused. At times you're going to be physically and mentally abused by other human beings, and you're not going to remember that these human beings are your closest angelic friends in disguise. You're not going to remember that they are only carrying out a plan of spiritual correction that you created for yourself. You're also going to see situations in which rape and murder occur, and you're going to believe that God no longer cares for His children. But there is nothing farther from the truth. The angels that are living on Earth in human form are totally loved by God, and because of His love for them, He allows the severest situations to occur on Earth. These situations occur so the angels can learn the lessons they need to learn. Every significant situation that occurs on Earth was planned by angels for their spiritual growth. The more severe the situation, the more willing was an angel to learn a particular spiritual lesson."

Jesus continued, "Every significant thing that happens on Earth is solely for the spiritual enhancement of the angels and is done with love and understanding. As a human, you won't recognize this fact, and you'll be tormented by the events as they occur. The torment, anger, and fear that you'll experience are required for the correction of your imperfection. If there was an easier way to correct your imperfection, it would be done, but we have found that life at Earth University provides the best overall results. When you go to Earth, a part of my spirit will go with you. My spirit, a Christ Consciousness, will be inside of you to help you in times of need. Just quiet your mind, pray for help, and believe that I will answer. The key to your prayers is in the <u>believing</u>."

Therefore I tell you, whatever you ask for in prayer, <u>believe</u> that you have received it, and it will be yours.

(Mark 11: 24)

So now, just about everything was ready for the trip. Marcus had decided to be a male Caucasion living in the United States in a lower-class neighborhood. It was agreed that no major events would happen in his life until he was 25 years old. Then during the next 10 years, several events would occur that would give him the opportunity to learn the things he needed to learn about forgiveness. During those years, he would blame himself and others for a daughter who dies in a car accident, for a marriage that fails, and for his inability to hold a job. The plan was well written, but how well the lessons about forgiveness would be learned would depend on Marcus' free will, his freedom to make his own choices while on Earth. If the lessons weren't learned during this visit to Earth University, another lifetime visit would be required in the future.

One additional detail was required before his trip to planet Earth could take place. It hadn't been decided what was going to happen once the lessons on forgiveness were learned. Marcus was well aware that there were two options available. The first option was to let his human body die immediately after learning the lessons and come straight home as a spirit to the universe, to a God Consciousness. This option is normally selected by most spirits, because it provides the quickest way to rejoin their angelic friends. The second option was to stay at Earth University and teach the lessons that Jesus was teaching while He was on the planet. Marcus decided to stay and teach on Earth for a few years before returning home.

All arrangements had now been completed. A perfect Divine Plan had been developed and approved. All the angels that were involved in the plan knew exactly what they had to do to make the plan work and were eagerly waiting to appear on Earth's stage to play their important roles. Every role, no matter how it would be perceived on Earth, would be performed with a deep spiritual love.

So angel Marcus came to Earth University to fulfill his Divine Plan. As mandated by the plan, the early part of his life was fairly normal. However, when he became 25 years old, his only daughter was killed in a car accident, for which he held himself responsible. He was driving the car while intoxicated and ran into a tree. She was the only fatality. When he was 28, his wife left him for another man. By the time he was 30, the pressures of life were so great that he was unable to hold a steady job and spent most of his time in a local bar. During those difficult years, he held himself responsible for most of his personal problems and could not forgive himself. After 10 years of unforgiveness, he became involved in a spiritual program and learned how to forgive himself and others.

Angel Marcus is now doing fine and is teaching classes on spirituality at Earth University. Someday in the near future he is expected to leave his human body and return to his angelic friends near the star of Kutume. This particular life cycle will then be completed. But after this lifetime, there will be another life to live on Earth for the purpose of correcting another minor imperfection. Each new life on planet Earth, however, will be more beautiful and peaceful than the previous, because in each life cycle, the lessons to be learned are less severe.

The end

Overview of life

The above story about angel Marcus presents an interesting alternative to the philosophy of life that is taught in many of our Christian churches and public schools. Reincarnation, the rebirth of the soul in another body, is becoming an acceptable explanation for many Christians who are searching for a deeper understanding of life. Whether or not you believe in reincarnation, however, shouldn't greatly affect the way you live your life. Your life should be lived in the manner that brings you the most happiness. God wants you to be happy as you live and learn on Earth.

When it's time to make significant changes in your lifestyle, your Higher Power, the God within, will let you know that the time has arrived by causing you physical and mental discomfort. If you are currently unhappy with the situations in your life, or if you have several physical ailments, it may be an indication that it's time to direct more attention to your life's real purpose, which is spiritual growth.

For those of you who enjoy reading statistics, you may be interested in obtaining the survey results of a Gallup Poll that was conducted in 1981 on spiritual beliefs. Reincarnation was addressed in this study. According to this large national poll, the number of Americans believing in the rebirth concept is increasing. In 1981, 23% of the American adults that were surveyed believed in reincarnation. In this investigation, 67% of the adults didn't believe in reincarnation and 10% had no opinion. It's interesting to note that based on this analysis, 25% of all Catholics and 21% of all Protestants believe in the rebirth of the soul into a new body after death. The survey also indicated that 29% of all adults under the age of 30 believe in the rebirth process. The purpose of this lesson is not to prove or disprove the concept of reincarnation, but to bring to your attention a belief that is accepted by a large portion of the general population.

A belief in reincarnation doesn't imply that your life is 100% predestined by God. Reincarnation and predestination are two very different concepts, and it may be possible to experience one without the other. In the dictionary, reincarnation is defined as "the doctrine that the soul reappears after death in another body," whereas predestination is "the doctrine that God foreordained everything that will happen in a particular life." Many people believe as I do, that reincarnation of the soul does occur, but only the most significant events in a particular lifetime are predestined. It has been suggested by some spiritual leaders that less than 10% of the activities in our lives are predestined, while the greater portion of our life experiences are created by our free wills.

If the spiritual concepts in the story about angel Marcus are true, and many believe they are, then the following points can be made:

- Your real purpose in life is to correct a minor imperfection in your soul. This correction will bring you closer to the "oneness" of God.

- You wouldn't be living on planet Earth if you didn't have a minor imperfection in your near-perfect soul to correct.

- All significant events that are happening in your life are for your spiritual growth.

- The planet Earth is a giant "university" that God has

created solely for the correction of imperfections in the soul. The Earth is a perfect place to learn spiritual lessons, because of its diversities and its adversities. All situations that occur on Earth are perfect.

- You are the creator of your own unique Divine Plan. You are also your own creation that is living out the plan. You designed every significant aspect of your life on Earth. You selected your parents and determined your childhood experiences before you were born.

- Human death occurs only when the spiritual purpose or purposes have been completed. Death isn't just the completion of a spiritual assignment on Earth, but it's also the start of a beautiful reunion with loving spiritual friends.

- Spiritual life is eternal. It has no beginning or end. Although the human body remains on Earth when you die, your Spiritual Being, your soul, returns to heaven and continues to live and grow.

The above statements seem almost anti-Christian to many of us who were raised as Christians. Yet the teachings of Jesus Christ don't contradict any of these statements. I personally believe that the statements are 100% accurate. It's estimated that over 20% of the world population currently accepts ideas similar to these in their daily spiritual practices. This is particularly true of the people living in the Eastern Hemisphere. You should believe whatever feels right to you. Let your Higher Power, the Holy Spirit within you, be your spiritual guide.

Until we recognize that life is not just something to be enjoyed, but rather a task that each of us is assigned, we'll never find meaning in our lives and we'll never be truly happy.

Victor Frankl

FOLLOW-UP EXERCISES

(1) What do you think your spiritual purposes are in this lifetime? Are you having difficulties in loving, forgiving, or trusting? Often the areas in which you're experiencing emotional pain are the areas in which your soul is crying for help. You won't be totally happy until you address these areas.

(2) Spend some quiet time thinking about reincarnation. Is it possible that our souls do reappear in other bodies after we die? Discuss your thoughts openly with some close friends.

—Day #5—

Discovering your Divine Plan

A few years ago I was giving a lecture on Spiritual Laws at a large church near Detroit. There were over a thousand people in the audience that particular day as I told a story about reincarnation and divine plans. The story was very similar to the one about Angel Marcus that we shared on Day 4. After the session was over, a man came up to me with a Bible in his hand and asked me if I really believed what I was telling the group. I told him that I wouldn't have told the story if I didn't believe it was true. So the man handed me the Bible and said that if the concepts of divine plans and reincarnation were in the Bible, he would believe in them. He said he was a good Christian and only believed in the teachings that were in the Bible. I gave his Bible back to him and politely asked him to see me during the coffee break. At that time I would show him exactly where in the Bible it talks about reincarnation and divine plans.

When it was time for a coffee break, I was ready to discuss the issues with the man. I had gone to my own Bible and found exactly what I needed to support my ideas. I was prepared to discuss with him how the lives of Jesus and John the Baptist were both part of a divine plan. I was also ready to talk about how the Bible describes John the Baptist as the reincarnated prophet Elijah. I was ready for the discussion, but the man never came back. In fact, I never saw him again.

Divine plans and reincarnation

Many of us aren't aware that there are such things as divine plans, even though the Bible does refer to them. By definition, a divine plan is an outline of events for a particular lifetime that has been preplanned by God for the purpose of fulfilling a spiritual need. Having divine plans doesn't mean that all events in our lives are 100% predestined by God. All it means is that certain events will occur in our lives in a "divine order" so that a "divine purpose" is satisfied. Some people are more comfortable referring to the divine plan as God's Will. This is fine, since the two are very similar. If you're living within your divine plan, you're also living a life based on God's Will. It's important to understand that most of the events in our lives are probably not part of our divine plans, but are the direct result of our own free wills.

The life of Jesus is probably the best documented example of living within a divine plan. Portions of His Divine Plan are described in the Old Testament as follows:

— Announced by John the Baptist. (Malachi 3:1, 4:5)
— Born in Bethlehem. (Micah 5:2)
— Born of a virgin. (Isaiah 7:14)
— People wept at the massacre of the infants of Bethlehem.
    (Jeremiah 31:15)
— Flight to Egypt. (Hosea 11:1)
— Triumphal entry. (Zechariah 9:9)
— Bought for 30 pieces of silver. (Zechariah 11:12-13)
— Pierced at crucifixion. (Zechariah 12:10)
— Crucified; a lamb for our sins. (Isaiah 53)
— Buried in a rich man's grave. (Isaiah 53)

The above events, which were predestined by God and recorded in the Bible hundreds of years before the birth of Jesus, became part of Jesus' Divine Plan. Unlike most of us, Jesus was aware of certain segments of His Divine Plan as He lived on Earth. This is clearly indicated by the discussions Jesus had with His disciples about the crucifixion, as well as other significant events, before they occurred.

Reincarnation is also alluded to in the Bible. Probably the best example is the passage where Jesus tells his disciples that the deceased spiritual leader Elijah has already reappeared on Earth in the form of John the Baptist. Elijah, who was a great prophet of Israel and had died several hundred years before the birth of John the Baptist, was expected to reappear on Earth before the Messiah came. The Bible, in Matthew 17:10-13, says:

His disciples asked, "Why do the Jewish leaders insist Elijah must return before the Messiah comes?" Jesus replied, "They are right. Elijah must come and set everything in order. And, in fact, he has already come, but he wasn't recognized and was badly mistreated by many. And I, the Messiah, shall also suffer at their hands." Then the disciples realized he was speaking of John the Baptist.

The Bible makes it perfectly clear that Jesus did believe in reincarnation. The Bible also makes it quite clear that divine plans did exist for Jesus and John the Baptist. Individual divine plans also exist for each of us. Our souls have created these divine plans for the purpose of correcting minor imperfections that are within them. Our purpose as human beings is to live out these plans so that the corrections can be made. These divine plans dictate that certain significant events will occur during our lives. It's from these events that our souls will grow and ultimately experience a closer "oneness" with God.

By living within your divine plan, imperfections in your soul will be corrected, and you'll experience a closer "oneness" with God.

Being aware of your divine plan

Although it's possible to determine some aspects of your divine plan, the majority of it is kept as a secret within your soul. If you were fully aware of your divine plan, then the major events that are scheduled to occur in your life to teach you spiritual lessons wouldn't be as dramatic. It would be similar to seeing a movie after being told the ending. The significant events in the movie would no longer have the proper emotional impact. In life, it's through experiences that have emotional impact that we learn the most difficult human lessons. In a similar manner, the growth of our souls is dependent on how we as humans perceive and react to situations in life. It's through our human reactions to human situations that our spiritual souls develop.

By just having an awareness that we're living within divine plans, and that life isn't as purposeless and as chaotic as it appears, has brought a great deal of inner peace to many people. By accepting the fact that everyone has a divine plan and that certain significant events will occur to teach us spiritual lessons, we become less fearful and reactive to life's difficult situations. Before I became aware of portions of my divine plan, I would often react in negative ways to undesirable events. I wouldn't necessarily become hostile, but I would unmercifully criticize myself and others, or I would lose confidence in my abilities and procrastinate. Now that I believe that many of the undesirable events in my life were actually planned by my soul to teach itself lessons, I just accept the events, learn the lessons, and move on with life. Although it's true that some events may still adversely affect me, I'll normally bounce right back, because I'm aware that I'm living within a divine plan that was designed with love. Once it's understood that we're all living within divine plans, life becomes a beautiful adventure, filled with love and lessons.

Once it's understood that we're all living within divine plans, life becomes a beautiful adventure, filled with love and lessons.

Discovering your divine plan

There are many ways to discover portions of your divine plan. Some of them are listed below:

(1) *Through meditations:* In my opinion, meditation is the most direct route for obtaining an awareness of your divine plan. During meditation, you can talk directly to your soul and ask questions about your unique plan. You may not get all the answers you want, but you will receive sufficient information.

(2) *Through prayers:* There are two ways in which prayers can indirectly help you discover your divine plan. The first is by noticing which prayers are answered, and the second is by being aware of which prayers aren't answered. Both of these responses by God can be significant indicators of your divine plan. As we discussed in an earlier lesson, God answers all prayers. His response, however, will not be in direct conflict with a divine plan. Therefore, if a particular prayer is not answered, it may be because it's in conflict with your divine plan or someone else's divine plan. If you pray that a sick friend doesn't die, and that person dies, be happy for that person and give thanks to God, since the divine plan of the individual that you prayed for was being honored. If you pray for something and get it, assume that what you got doesn't conflict with your divine plan, and that maybe, it's even part of it.

(3) *Through personal desires and interests:* Personal desires

and interests are also strong indicators of your divine plan. When your divine plan was being created by your soul, your soul scheduled activities for your early childhood that would determine the type of personality and belief system you would develop. Your soul made sure that your adult personality and belief system would be compatible with your divine plan. In other words, if your divine plan states you're to become a nurse or a medical doctor, your personality and beliefs would have been developed in such a way that you would have an overwhelming desire to help people. On the other hand, if you are to learn your spiritual lessons on Earth in the role of an uncaring business executive, your personality and beliefs would have been developed through situations that involved fear and insecurity. It's probably safe to say that whatever provides you with a deep, fulfilling sense of love and happiness is part of your divine plan.

(4) *Through intuitive feelings:* What you intuitively feel is also a good indicator of your divine plan. This is because your soul speaks directly to you through your intuition. Your intuition has nothing to do with your rational thought process. It's unfortunate that many of us allow our rational minds to greatly overpower our intuitive feelings. It's generally agreed that most intellectuals would be much happier and more successful in life if they would rely more on their intuitive feelings.

(5) *Through intellectual thoughts:* Your divine plan can also be revealed to you through your intellectual thoughts. Your God-given mind has the ability to examine all of the events that have occurred in your life and to draw an accurate conclusion about your divine plan. Once you intellectually understand portions of your divine plan, you can create future situations that are consistent with it by employing the spiritual Law of Thought.

(6) *Through uncommon occurrences:* Often we gain insights about our divine plans in the most unusual ways. A stranger may call you on the phone and give you the special information you needed to make a major decision. You may wake up in the middle of the night and hear a meaningful message when no one else is around. You may be playing a record and it keeps getting stuck on

a certain word. You may be in a library and find that somehow a particular book has ended up on your desk, and when you browse through it, you discover it contains exactly what you needed to know. You may see a vision of a person who had died years earlier, and it sparks a spiritual awakening. Whether or not we're listening, our souls are continuously talking to us and trying to make it easy for us to follow our divine plans. Many of us have already learned that the more we're in tune with our divine plans, the more happiness we experience in life.

The more we're in tune with our divine plans, the more happiness we experience in life.

Segments of the author's divine plan

The last five years of my life have been filled with many strange occurrences. Some of these experiences have given me insights to my divine plan. Based on my own personal analysis, which could be 100% wrong, my soul is here on Earth to work on forgiveness and trust. I believe my soul has had difficulty in the past forgiving others and itself for things that have previously occurred and, therefore, is back on Earth to relearn some lessons on forgiveness. I also believe my soul is here to rediscover the importance of trusting God and His Divine Wisdom. Upon completing these lessons, I believe my divine plan states that I will stay on Earth for awhile and be a teacher.

My main lesson on forgiveness began in 1972 when my first wife committed suicide. This event caused me a tremendous amount of mental pain. I couldn't forgive her for what she had done, and I couldn't forgive myself for not helping her more with her illness. Then in the spring of 1986, after having endured 14 years of limited happiness, I was finally able to open my heart and forgive the two of us. The forgiveness process started during a men's spiritual retreat weekend. At the retreat a gifted minister,

Rev. Jack Boland, helped me to understand that my wife and I really had done the very best we could at that particular time and, therefore, shouldn't be blamed for the tragic event. With this new understanding, I was able to forgive. The act of forgiveness released me from a very heavy burden.

Three months later my deceased wife of 14 years visited me. Although I have already told you this story, I would like to repeat it, because it was this experience that changed the direction of my life. When she visited me, I was lying in bed thinking about the day's activities. It was a hot summer night, and I remember the windows being open. As I lay there on my back, staring at the ceiling, she appeared at the foot of the bed. I could only see her from the waist up. She looked just as I remembered her, except her hair was longer. It was the length when we first met. We talked, but not with words. Somehow we communicated through our minds. She said, "Hello, David. Are you at peace?" And I said, "Yes." She said, "That's good. I just wanted to tell you that you're doing a great job raising our son." I said, "Thank you." Then she left. I lay there for about an hour thinking about the experience before I fell asleep. That experience, which was very peaceful and assuring, was the catalyst for my spiritual awakening.

Another interesting event occurred in the spring of 1987 while I was taking a Dale Carnegie course in human relations. One of my assignments for the last class was to prepare a two minute talk, in which I would share a future goal and describe how I would achieve it. The night before the class I prepared some mental notes about the goal, which was to start my own consulting company. I knew exactly what I wanted to say about this important goal and rehearsed it several times before class. During class the instructor passed out 3x5 cards and asked each of us to write one of our main goals and describe how we were going to achieve it. To my amazement, without really thinking, I wrote the following words, "My goal is to become a minister, and I'll do this by quitting the company that I'm working for, teach spiritual classes at the church, and become involved with the church's board of directors." After I finished writing, I looked at what I wrote and started to smile in astonishment. I had never consciously considered becoming a minister. At that very moment the instructor yelled out, "Dave Lindsey, please come up to the front of the room and tell the rest of the students about your goal." I went up in front of the other 43 students and was speechless. Then I told the class that I had no idea why I wrote what I wrote. The instructor asked me if I really wanted to become a minister and to my surprise I said, "Yes." I wasn't even sure why I was saying what I was saying, but it felt so right. I now believe what was happening in front of the whole class was that part of my divine plan, my hidden agenda for life, was being exposed.

Four months later, after 17 years as an engineer and product planner for General Motors, I left the company and started my own consulting firm. My new company was a success right from the start. A few months later, I was also teaching spiritual classes in my spare time. The teaching experience felt very natural and was extremely satisfying. I was aware that everything in my life at this particular time was working out perfectly, just as if it had been planned. But I didn't know why. My ego said, "I'm doing it all." But my intuition said, "God is working through you." I now know that my intuition was correct.

A few months later, I took a course in meditation. This course had a major effect on my life, because it opened the door to a two-way communication with Spirit. Although it took several months to learn how to deeply meditate, I finally did learn. It has been through meditation that I have obtained a great deal of information about life.

In January of 1988, I believe that God tested my human desire for material wealth. Based on my performance as a marketing consultant, I was offered a position of Vice President of Sales and Marketing for a fairly large Virginia company. With this position came all the "toys" of an executive, plus a huge salary and a substantial bonus. The job offer was very tempting, and my wife and I spent many hours discussing it. I was about ready to accept the position when I received a phone call from a stranger who had seen me on TV a few weeks earlier talking about spiritual principles. The man, who was very spiritual, identified himself as Jesse. Jesse told me that he didn't know why he was calling me, but that he felt drawn to do so. About ten minutes into the conversation, Jesse suddenly stopped talking and said, "I have a message for you from God." He told me that God wanted to work through me, and that the change I was considering, I shouldn't make. At the particular time Jesse said this, he wasn't aware that I was about ready to accept a new job. We spent seven hours that weekend talking on the phone, and by the end of the weekend, I was convinced I wasn't suppose to take the job. I declined the job offer the following week. I have never met Jesse face-to-face, but I believe he is a special person that God uses to deliver messages to those of us who are having problems listening to our own inner guidance. Jesse helped me to discover a portion of my divine plan.

Since the phone call from Jesse, I have learned that our souls speak to us in many ways. One of the ways they get our attention is by giving us messages in the middle of the night when our mental activities are slow. It's at this time that our intellectual minds are at rest and are unable to interfere with divine messages. I have been awakened many times about three o'clock in the morning and given messages. Most of the time the messages come from a soft, inner voice. Twice, however, the voice has been loud and seemed to come from within the room. On those two occasions the voice has said, "A step beyond" and "In order to have credibility in man's world, you must have a reverend's title." Although the second message is clear, I'm not sure what the first message means. I have asked for clarification of the first message in meditation, but haven't received it yet. When it's time to know, I'm sure I'll be told.

The strangest spiritual event that has occurred to me so far happened on March 12, 1988. It occurred about four o'clock in the morning. I woke up from a deep sleep with a feeling that something or someone was in the room. I lay in bed without moving for several seconds and just listened for noises. There were none, so I turned and looked over my shoulder. To my amazement, there was a large sparkling silver cloud in the room. The cloud appeared to be about a foot thick and about five feet in diameter. Although I was at peace with the event, I remember thinking that this was how I was going to make my transition back to heaven. I said to the cloud, "God, if that is you, just take me." The glittering cloud moved above me, and my whole body started to sparkle. This occurred for several minutes, and then the cloud either went away or went into my body. I lay in bed for about an hour in a very peaceful state after the cloud disappeared. Then I went back to sleep. Was it all a dream, or did it really occur? I remember too many of the details of the occurrence to think it was a dream. Was

I being told something about my divine plan? I'm not sure. I will say that since the experience, my intuition and understanding of situations in life have become much clearer.

Several months later, I had another interesting experience. I was discussing spiritual principles with a group of women who were having marital and family problems. During the session, one of the ladies complained about severe back pains that she had been having for about two months. As I was talking to the group, an inner voice said, "You can heal her." I tried to ignore the voice, but it kept on coming back. At the end of the session when no one else was around, I told the lady what the inner voice had said. I told her I had never healed anyone and I didn't know what to do except hold her and pray. She was willing to try it, so I put my arms around her and prayed that God would heal her. When I was done, I asked her how she felt, and she said she didn't feel any better. About a month later when my wife and I were at church together, I saw the lady again. She came running over to us and told me that when she got up the next morning after the healing event, she no longer had any pains in her back. She said she had written in her diary that "Rev. Lindsey had healed her." That afternoon I went into meditation and asked about spiritual healing, and was told that I personally had no powers to heal anyone, but since I was willing to allow God to work through me, some healings would take place in my presence. I was also told that the decisions concerning who would be healed would be made solely by God and would be based upon spiritual needs. Was this healing event another indication that my divine plan states that I'll become a spiritual teacher? I think so.

I would like to end this lesson with the most beautiful message I have ever received during a meditation. It came about a year ago on a day that my ego was overactive. Normally while in deep meditation, I'm not aware of any parts of my body. My only awareness is that my mind is communicating with a loving Spirit. However, during this particular meditation as I heard the message, I felt tears of joy running down my cheeks. The message really moved me. I know that since we're all sons and daughters of the same loving God, the message wasn't meant for me exclusively, but is for all of us. The message was: "My beloved son, you're a child of God and you'll always be loved and protected."

*As children of a loving God,
we're totally loved and
protected at all times.*

FOLLOW-UP EXERCISES

(1) Do you have any intuitive feelings about your divine plan? Has there ever been a major change in your personality or belief system as a result of an unusual experience? Write on a sheet of paper what you think your divine plan might include.

(2) You have all the God-given talents and skills you need to live a happy life. Your divine plan was designed that way. Make a list of your talents and skills, and then circle those that aren't being fully utilized. Are there good reasons why you're not using some of your talents?

—Day #6—

Developing a relationship with God

When I was attending a college in Cleveland in the 1960's, I met a very interesting man from Pakistan. He had a strange name that most of us couldn't pronounce, so we called him Bennie. Bennie was one of those people that everyone enjoyed being around. He was always happy and smiling. He was charismatic, charming, and fun-loving. When the time was right, he always had a funny joke to tell. But more importantly, he was deeply sincere and projected a great deal of warmth and unconditional love. Bennie even kept a list of his friends' birthdays and would always make sure those special days didn't go by unnoticed. Although he didn't seem to have a lot of money, he always had a small gift or card for those special occasions. When someone was worried or depressed, Bennie was always there to brighten their day. He had the personality that most of us dream of having. Because of the joy Bennie brought to our group, none of us seemed to mind the inconvenience of his wheelchair.

One day several of us were sitting in the school lounge talking about our future goals and how much happier we would probably be once we completed school, when someone turned to Bennie and asked in an untactful manner, "How can you be so happy knowing that you'll probably be in a wheelchair for the rest of your life?" We were all stunned and very embarrassed by the blunt question. Bennie, however, was not bothered by it, and in fact, wondered why he was never asked the question before. He then told us a brief story about his life.

Bennie told us that he was one of eight children of a very influential family in Pakistan. He told us that because of the great wealth and love within his family, he could have anything he wanted just by asking his father for it. He told us the reason he was so happy all the time was because he always felt very secure and protected. It became obvious to us as we listened to Bennie, that he truly believed his parents' wealth and love would help him overcome the critical situations in his life. He told us that as far as being in a wheelchair for the rest of his life, it really didn't matter that much to him, because the people who were important to him would accept him for what he felt in his heart and wouldn't reject him because of his physical limitations. I remember by the end of his story how much I admired him for his ability to see beyond his apparent physical constraints. On the other hand, I also remember having a concern about how much of his happiness was directly tied to his parents' wealth and love.

It was about a year after that discussion that Bennie's personality greatly changed. Instead of being fun-loving and happy, he was usually depressed and filled with self-pity. He no longer projected the sincerity and warmth he once did. He was oversensitive and manipulative, and often blamed many of us for his daily problems. Bennie wasn't the same Bennie we had grown to love and admire.

I talked to Bennie one day about the changes we had noticed in him. At first he denied there were any changes, and said the real problem was that we were just tired of pushing him around in his wheelchair. As we sat there, however, he started to tell me what was really bothering him. He told me his father had recently made some unwise financial investments in Pakistan and had lost most of the family's wealth. He also told me he had received a letter from his brother that said their father had become emotionally unstable as a result of the stress caused by the unfavorable investments. Bennie said he was worried about his future and no longer felt the deep love and protection he once did from his father. As I listened to Bennie, I became aware of the emotional pain he was experiencing. I remember thinking at that time about how a person, who was greatly admired for his optimistic attitude towards life, had changed so much in one year. Although I didn't understand exactly what was happening to Bennie, I felt compassion for him. Now as I look back at Bennie's difficult situation, I see a major mistake that Bennie had made. He had put all his faith in the protective love of an earthly father instead of a heavenly father. If Bennie's original inner security and happiness had been based on God's protective love, Bennie could have maintained his positive attitude throughout the family's difficult situation.

Although Bennie's story is unique, the feelings and thoughts he experienced during that difficult time in his life are common. Many of us today have those same empty, insecure feelings. Bennie was learning a valuable lesson about life, and that is, to be truly happy, a person must experience deep feelings of love and inner security. Bennie did at one time experience these feelings. However, the foundation for his feelings was unstable. Bennie had put all his faith for a happy life in his relationship with his family. Relationships with family and friends are never totally stable. We like to think they are, but they are not. Many of us are learning from our daily experiences that there aren't any completely stable and lasting relationships between earthly entities. Look at every one of your relationships and see how fragile and unstable they really are. At any particular moment, a loving human relationship can be greatly diminished by the death of a spouse, a child, or a friend. At any particular moment a meaningful relationship with a material object such as a house, a car, or a business can be destroyed by a fire. If your happiness is dependent on a relationship with anything else but God, you'll never obtain lasting happiness. The only truly stable relationship you'll ever have will be the loving relationship you have with God. Let me repeat that for emphasis. *The only truly stable relationship you'll ever have will be the loving relationship you have with God.* Earth University was purposely designed that way, so that we would develop loving relationships with the Creator.

Developing a loving relationship with God is the most important thing you'll ever do. Two thousand years ago, Jesus told us the most important rule for living is to love God. In the Bible, in Matthew 22:37,38, Jesus said,

You shall love the Lord your God with all your heart, with all your soul, and with all your mind. This is the first and greatest commandment.

If you want to be truly happy in life, develop a loving relationship with God. Once you do this, you'll feel total joy in your life, and no situation on Earth will ever greatly disturb you.

The only truly stable relationships that can ever exist are the loving relationships we have with God. It's these relationships that bring us lasting happiness.

Who is God?

Many of us have difficulty developing a conscious relationship with God, because we don't know who or what God is. And what makes it more frustrating is the fact that none of the experts on religious doctrines can totally agree on a definition for God. If you ask your local priests, ministers, and rabbis who God is, you'll get a wide range of answers. There seems to be a great mystery to God's true identity.

In the dictionary, God is defined as follows:

God: The creator and ruler of the universe; regarded as eternal, all-powerful, all-knowing, and infinite.

This is an excellent starting point for obtaining a basic understanding of God. So let's generate specific definitions for each of the descriptive words.

As creator of the universe, we're saying that God brought into existence everything that is currently visible and invisible in the universe. This means that God was the controlling force behind the "Big Bang" that occurred 16 billion years ago when the universe was formed. This also implies that God has been active since the initial creation and is directly responsible for the creation of your current visible body, as well as your invisible soul.

As supreme ruler of the universe, God has complete authority over the actions, conducts, and procedures of all things that exist. This means that God is actively involved in the activities of every human being on Earth.

Being eternal means there is no beginning or end to God. God is everlasting and forever the same. This means that God will always exist and is present right now in our lives. Being eternal implies that God is unchanging and is always true and valid. This means that what Jesus taught us about God two thousand years ago is still true today. We have been blessed with a loving God.

Being all-powerful means that God has unlimited ability to do or produce whatever He desires. Because of His many powers, He can perform an unlimited number of miracles for His children.

Being all-knowing means that God has a clear perception and understanding of everything that is occurring within His universe. This implies that God is well aware of everything you do and think. God actually knows your needs and desires before you pray for them. You have no secrets from God.

God is infinite means more than just the fact that God has no limits or bounds. It also implies that the true definition of God is beyond the comprehension of the human mind. We can only define God with terms we can understand, but God is much greater than this.

Although the dictionary definition of God is fairly good in general terms, I would like to add two more descriptive words to our definition to make it more accurate. The words are from the Bible and are "love" and "spirit." In the New Testament, we're told the following:

> God is a Spirit.   (John 4:24)
> God is love.   (1 John 4:8)

By adding these words to our previous definition of God, we obtain the following general definition. *God is a loving Spirit that created and rules the universe. This Spirit is eternal, all-powerful, all-knowing, and infinite.*

Many people believe there is much more to God than what is stated above, and they are correct. God is much more. The purpose of this simple exercise wasn't to convince you that the definition presented here about God is the total truth and should be accepted without modifications. The purpose of this exercise was to create a strong desire within you to identify in your own heart who God is. Whatever your intuitive feelings are about God, you should just accept them for now. Your soul, in time, may guide you to a different definition.

God is a loving Spirit that created and rules the universe. This Spirit is eternal, all-powerful, all-knowing, and infinite.

Developing your own definition of God

If God wanted us to know His exact identity, I'm sure He would find a creative way of telling us. Maybe His artistic style would be to rearrange the stars so they would spell out a divine message. Or maybe He would have the Earth stop rotating for a few hours, and during that time of crisis, appear and fill our hearts with love and peace. I personally don't think anything like this is going to happen. I believe God wants us to discover Him for ourselves by using our God-given intellectual minds and intuitive hearts.

It wouldn't be truthful for me to say I know who God is, because I don't. I know many things about God from my recent experiences, but my knowledge of Him is extremely limited. I'm sure He is much greater than I could ever imagine.

When I was a young boy, I was told that God was a powerful old man with a long white beard who sat on a throne in heaven, and on His right side stood Jesus, and on His left side stood a man with a white sheet over his body. This sheeted man was the Holy Ghost. I was told that these three people were watching everything I did, and I would only go to heaven if I obeyed their religious laws. I was also told that when I heard thunder, it wasn't anything to worry about, because it was just God walking around, or that He and Jesus were bowling. As a child, my perception of God was extremely distorted.

When I was in my twenties and thirties, I believed God didn't exist or, if He did, He wasn't interested in my personal activities. During this stage of my life, I hardly ever thought about God. I was more interested in self-discipline and doing "my own thing." Those were very difficult years for me.

Now that I'm in my forties, I have a completely different view about God. Because I have talked to Him many times in meditation and have seen Him perform many miracles in my life, I know without a doubt that He exists and is active in my life. I currently believe that God, the Heavenly Father, is a loving Spirit that permeates the whole universe. By permeating objects in the universe, I'm saying that His energy or spirit flows through them and affects every part of them. I perceive God as a powerful energy force that permeates, penetrates, and/or exists in all things in the universe. In my mind, God isn't all things, but is in all things.

What do you believe about God? And why do you believe what you do? Unfortunately, many of us are too busy to think about God's true identity and, therefore, just accept the beliefs that are presented to us by our parents or by a neighborhood church. It's interesting to note that most of us who are American Christians are such, only because we were born in America to Christian parents. For many of us, we inherited our spiritual beliefs. Our current thoughts about God would probably be completely different if we were born in another country such as India, China, or Japan. Isn't it time to decide for yourself who God really is? Your decision about God's identity and your personal relationship with Him will have a major effect on your overall happiness.

In order to help you discover God's identity, I have listed the following biblical quotes and facts.

1. God is a Spirit. (John 4:24)
2. God is love. (1 John 4:8)
3. Our God is full of compassion. (Psalms 116:5)
4. God is not a man. (Numbers 23:19)
5. There is one God, and one mediator between God and men, the man Jesus Christ. (1 Timothy 2:5)
6. Christ is the Son of God. (Acts 8:37)
7. We are God's children right now. (1 John 3:2)
8. Your body is a temple [home] of the Holy Spirit, who is in you, whom you have received from God. (1 Corinthians 6:19)
9. Jesus never said He was God, but that He was the Son of God and the Son of Man.
10. The Bible does not say anything about the doctrine of the Trinity, which states: There are three persons in the God-head of the Orthodox Christian Church: the Father, the Son, and the Holy Spirit, and that these three are one God, the same in substance, equal in power and glory. The doctrine of the Trinity, which states that Jesus is God, was written by a group of men over one hundred years after Jesus died. This doctrine was not formally accepted by the Christian Church until the fourth century. Before that

time, Jesus was considered just the Son of God, not God.

The more I read the Bible, and the more I learn about the awesome powers of the early Christian church leaders, the more I wonder if our Christian teachings are totally valid. I honestly don't know what is true. Is Jesus the Son of God or God? Was Jesus able to perform the miracles He did, because He is God, or because when He was on Earth as a man, he was filled with the Spirit of God? When Jesus said, "I and my Father are one" (John 10:30), was He saying that He and the Father are God, or was He referring to the "oneness" of a single God Spirit that permeates the universe? What was Jesus trying to tell us when He said, "By myself I can do nothing." (John 5:30)? What was Jesus implying when He said, "It is the Father living in me that is doing the work. Believe me when I say that I am in the Father and the Father is in me." (John 14:10,11). I'm not sure exactly what all these statements mean. What do you think? And why do you think what you do? Is it possible that some of us are focusing too much attention on God's messenger and not enough on His message of love and peace?

Being a good Christian

As president of a professional consulting firm, I have had the opportunity to meet many business executives from around the world. Most of the people I have met have been very friendly and a real pleasure to work with. There was one man, however, who tested the limits of my business diplomacy. Because he was aware of my spiritual interests, he used to tell me stories that would suggest that he was a good Christian. He told me that he went to church every Sunday, was an usher twice a month, and gave 10% of his personal earnings to the church. Because of this, he truly believed he was a good Christian. In my opinion, although I know it's wrong to judge others, he wasn't a good Christian. I say this, because it seemed as if he was living his life without love and respect for others. Many people feared him, because of his cruel and vicious assaults on his colleagues and friends. He once told me that the worth of a man is measured by the color of his skin and the number of coins in his pocket. Fortunately, we had a very short business relationship.

What is a good Christian? To answer this, we must first determine what a Christian is. The dictionary gives the following definitions.

1. a person having the qualities demonstrated and taught by Jesus Christ, such as love, kindness, respect, and decency.
2. a person believing in the teachings of Jesus Christ.
3. a person professing belief in Jesus as the Christ.
4. a decent, respectable person.
5. a person belonging to a Christian church.
6. anyone born of Christian parents.

These definitions are really quite different. Which one do you believe is most correct? The executive we discussed above might select number five. If Jesus came back to Earth today, which one do you think He would select? I personally think Jesus would select the first definition. He would probably tell us that a good Christian is a person who both believes and lives a life based on His teachings. He may even tell us that the formalities, rituals, dogmas, and traditions that burden our church services today are not necessary for our spiritual growth, and that we should rely more on the Holy Spirit, our Christ Consciousness, for daily direction.

Experiencing God

I have a special friend who is an architect. This man is very creative and is well known for his unique house designs. Recently, I visited his home and was overwhelmed by the beauty and creativity that was displayed in every room of his house. Everything was designed and built to perfection. As I walked through his house, I experienced the creative genius of my brilliant friend.

In a similar manner by living on Earth we automatically experience the perfection, creativity, and uniqueness of God. It's impossible to live anywhere in the universe and not experience God. God is everywhere and in everything. Everything that we sense with our five basic senses was created by God. The smell of a rose, the sound of a child laughing, the touch of a loved one, the colors of the trees in autumn, and the taste of honey were all created by God. Our intuitive power, our sixth sense, was also designed and created by God to help us more fully understand our existence on Earth. God has made it easy for us to experience Him.

The best way to experience God is to unconditionally love all things. Through the act of loving, we experience God, because as the Bible says, "God is love." The love that we feel for anything at any particular moment is God in action. Our love for a pet, a flower, or for any other material object is an experience of God. One of God's desires is for us to feel loved. And the only way we can feel loved is by giving love to others. When we withhold love from others, we withhold love from ourselves. The Law of Cause and Effect that we discussed on Day 3, clearly controls the amount of love we'll receive in life. We will be blessed with the same amount of love that we're willing to send out to others. Look at the people in your life who are deeply admired and loved. They are the people who are sending love to others.

How much <u>unconditional</u> love are you giving to others? Most people say they find it easy to love another person as long as the other person behaves in a proper manner. But who is to judge what is proper and what is not? Who among us can honestly say that one race is better than another or that one religion is more holy than another? We're not on Earth to make these types of judgments. The love we give to others must be unconditional, if we're to truly experience God. If you want a life filled with the awareness of God, live a life filled with love.

God is love. Whoever lives in love lives in God, and God in him.

1 John 4:16

To love ourselves is not selfish or egotistical, but an important way to express God's love. When we're filled with true self-love and honoring the Higher Power within us, we're experiencing God. To love ourselves is the second most important way of expressing God's love. First we're to love God, then ourselves, and then others. This is what Jesus was telling us when He said,

Love the Lord your God with all your heart and with all your soul and with all your mind. This is the first and greatest commandment. And the second is like it: Love your neighbor as yourself.

Jesus was telling us more than just the importance of love. He was telling us that before we can love our neighbors, we must be able to love ourselves. The degree we can love others is limited by the degree we love ourselves. It's important that we take time to fall in love with ourselves.

God can be directly experienced in many other ways. We have already discussed in earlier lessons the importance of prayer and meditation as ways to communicate directly with God. Another way God communicates with us is through the written word. By reading spiritual books, we can experience God. There have been many writings that have been inspired by God. Because of our human nature, however, we have a tendency to believe that only the books honored by our particular religion were inspired by God. But the truth is, most of the books about God and spirituality were inspired by Him. The Bible, the Koran, and the Bhagavad Gita were all inspired by God, and are all equally beneficial to the people who believe in their teachings. Many of the books we find in the religious sections of libraries were inspired by God. Even this book that you're reading right now, that is causing you to think more about God, was inspired by God. I never planned on writing this book, but was told to do so in meditation.

Another way we experience God is by having faith. Faith is the unquestioning belief that does not require proof or evidence. When we have difficulty finding a rational basis for believing that there is a God and a spiritual world, but still believe in them, we're demonstrating faith, and at the same time experiencing God. Being involved in a miracle that has occurred as a direct result of our faith is also an experience of God. The more faith we have in God, the more we'll experience Him. The more we believe, the more we'll see. Saint Augustine said, "Faith is to believe what we do not see, and the reward of this faith is to see what we believe."

Faith is to believe what we do not see, and the reward of this faith is to see what we believe.

Augustine

There are hundreds of other ways to experience God. Just by taking a walk in the woods, we see many examples of His natural laws. If we look through a telescope and view the heavenly bodies within our solar system, we find His perfect balance and order. If we look through the most powerful electron microscope and view His smallest creations, we find His perfection. God has made it easy for us to experience Him. He is all around us.

FOLLOW-UP EXERCISES

(1) How much of your happiness is tied directly to a relationship with another person? If that person died or left you, how quickly would you recover? How quickly would you become a "whole person"?

(2) Write on a sheet of paper your definition of God. How much of your happiness is based on your relationship with Him? Do you believe that God wants you to experience Him?

—Day #7—

Accepting the blessing of death

Earlier this year I had a routine physical examination by a young doctor at a local medical clinic. It was the first time I had met the doctor and was impressed by his general knowledge and mannerisms. He seemed to be a very warm and caring person. During the examination, he asked me if I had any medical problems. I told him I had occasional back pains and a minor blood disorder that I had been living with during the past 20 years. He told me we would discuss the disorder when the results from the blood tests were available.

A week later, I received a call from my new doctor and was asked to come back to his office as soon as possible. When I arrived at the clinic, the doctor's nurse asked me to wait for the doctor in his private office. So I went to his office and waited. Shortly after, the doctor came in and closed the door behind him. Then he turned to me and said, "I have just reviewed your blood test results and have a great concern. Are you aware that you have a major blood disorder and could die tomorrow?" I wasn't disturbed by his comments, since I had heard similar statements in the past from two other doctors. I smiled and acknowledged that I was aware of my blood disorder. Then with sincerity I said to him, "Isn't it true that you or my son or my wife could also die tomorrow? Isn't it true that we all are terminal and, therefore, will die someday in the near future?" I then told the doctor that I wasn't really that concerned about my blood disorder because I knew that people never actually died, but made "transitions" from this life to another life, which is even more beautiful.

At first the doctor didn't believe my comments, and told me I was in denial of my medical problems. He told me that everyone fears death, because death is an unknown. He informed me that his text books on death describe how terminal patients would go through several stages of denial and anger before they finally accepted the fact that they were going to die. He told me he thought I was in one of those stages. He indicated to me that maybe my spiritual beliefs were getting in the way of his sound medical judgement. He then suggested I begin taking some new experimental medicines to counteract my blood disorder.

It was obvious to me I was discussing a medical problem with a man who had an honest concern for my well-being, but who was only responding to my problem from his medical knowledge and not from a spiritual consciousness. So I asked the doctor for his honest opinion about when I was going to die. He said that based on his medical background he wasn't sure. It could be tomorrow, next year, or 50 years from now. I told him that based on my spiritual awareness, I had reached the same conclusion. I could make my transition back to heaven tomorrow, next year, or 50 years from now. However, I wouldn't be making the transition until my spiritual purpose for being on Earth was completed. Therefore, I told him I wouldn't be taking any special experimental medicines.

As I left his office, I'm sure the doctor thought I was some type of spiritual fanatic who was in great denial of a life threatening medical problem. I'm sure the doctor thought that someday he would read in the local paper that I had died prematurely from an untreated blood disorder, and that many of my family members and friends cried at the funeral. That story may someday appear in the paper, but it won't be the real truth about my transition. The true story would read something like this:

Dr. David Lindsey received one of God's greatest blessings today and made his transition back home to God's heavenly kingdom. His soul, which left his human body while he was fishing, floated peacefully through the tunnel of eternal love back to heaven. His soul was met there by several old friends. There were two beautiful ceremonies for the spiritual teacher, one on Earth and one in heaven. The one on Earth was attended by many loving friends dressed in colorful clothes. His friends first comforted each other and then joyously celebrated the completion of Dr. Lindsey's spiritual assignments on Earth. The ceremony in heaven was held near the star of Raphael and was attended by many angels in white robes. The angels were some of Dr. Lindsey's closest angelic friends who had made their transitions from Earth many years earlier. Dr. Lindsey's transition was as exciting and as beautiful as he had told people to expect.

What is death?

There are several natural phenomena that occur in this world that are extremely difficult to understand with our limited intellects. Because of our inabilities to comprehend the complexities of these events, we as humans often disagree about what the occurrences really mean. Since we have a tendency to fear the unknown, many of us create in our minds simplified pictures of what the occurrences represent and then seek out groups of people who have similar beliefs. This need to group together with people of common beliefs for the purpose of reducing our own anxieties is one of the reasons we have so many religions in this world. Death is one of these natural phenomena that we as humans have a difficult time understanding. I doubt if any of us are capable of fully understanding the purpose and complexity of death. Death of the human body, however, is a necessary part of God's plan for unity and therefore, none of us will ever escape it.

The dictionary definitions for death can't be applied to the transition of the soul from Earth to heaven, which is what most people believe death is. According to the dictionary, death is the following:

1.   Permanent ending of all life in a person, animal, or plant.

2.   Total extinction or destruction of anything.

These dictionary definitions of death are definitely not spiritual in nature. To think that God would create the spiritual component of man in His own image and likeness, and then permanently end His creation by total destruction, does not make any sense to an intellectual person or to a spiritual person. There must be more to the picture than what we can sense with our five basic senses. The truth is, most of the world's population believe there is a great deal more to death.

The spiritual definitions for human death are quite different than those found in the dictionary. Most spiritual people would probably accept one of the following definitions for human death.

1.   The transition of the soul from Earth to heaven.
2.   A passing from human life to spiritual life.
3.   The continuation of life without the human body.
4.   The soul's release from human restrictions.
5.   The doorway to an endless spiritual journey.
6.   The time at which the human body ceases to function.

Most of the religions in this world teach us that life continues after the human body stops functioning. Most religions recognize the fact that there is a spiritual entity within each human body, and this spiritual entity continues to live after the death of the human body. The Bible tells us that we have two parts to us, a human part and a spiritual part. The Bible says in 1 Corinthians 15:44:

There is a natural body and there is a spiritual body.

In the Bible, it also says that the human body dies and the spiritual body returns to God. In Ecclesiastes 12:7, the Bible states:

Then shall the dust [the human body] return to the Earth as it was, and the spirit [soul] shall return unto God who gave it.

There are clearly two parts to our total being. In this book, I have been referring to the two parts as the Human Being component and the Spiritual Being component. It really doesn't matter what we call them. The fact is, the human being component (the human body and ego) does stops functioning at the time we call death, however, the Spiritual Being component, the soul, continues to live. Our souls are truly eternal and never die. The sweetness of our personalities, the parts of us that people have grown to love and enjoy, continues to live within our souls.

Only the human body stops functioning at the time of death. Our Spiritual Beings, our souls, continue to live forever.

Purpose of death

The main purpose of death is to free the soul from the human restrictions it has accumulated while on Earth, so that it can peacefully return home to the heavens. The restrictions it leaves behind are the limiting human body and the maladjusted human ego. The death of the human body and ego is a perfect way to free the soul from the human characteristics that have caused it so many problems while existing on Earth. In many ways, human death can be viewed as the rebirth of the soul for a spiritual life in heaven. This is the reason that many of us consider death to be a blessing from God. Who among us wants to carry into the next life all the unresolved human problems we have created during this lifetime? If we truly believe we have a loving, merciful God with unlimited wisdom and power, we should feel comfortable knowing that our God has developed a perfect system for our souls' transitions from this life to another.

The timing of death

In God's perfect universe there are no accidents. Our all-knowing and all-powerful God is in complete control and, therefore, has been directly involved in all events that have occurred. Everything that has happened in the past and will occur in the future is part of God's spiritual plan for unity. No human death has ever occurred without the soul's decision to return home to the heavens. All human fatalities are the result of spiritual plans, which have been created and managed by individual souls. I understand that these last few statements are extremely difficult for many of us to accept, but I believe they are true. To think anything else, would be limiting God's mercifulness and powers, and would be suggesting that God doesn't care about His children's daily well-being.

When your soul decided many years ago to be incarnated into your current human body, it also decided at that time which of its imperfections it was going to rectify during its visit to Earth University. The divine plan that was developed by your soul was not designed to address all of its imperfections, but just a select few. Once these specific imperfections were corrected, the soul would then return to heaven. This return to heaven would take place at the time of human death.

When death occurs, it doesn't mean that the soul of a particular person is now perfect. It only means that the soul of that person has completed its spiritual assignments on Earth and has decided to return home. All spiritual assignments are designed so that the soul will be able to experience a greater degree of love once it returns to heaven. The majority of the assignments probably address such things as the soul's difficulty to feel or express love, intimacy, and forgiveness. Or maybe, the assignments are about trusting and having faith.

Some spiritual assignments are designed to help other souls along their spiritual paths. The death of a baby is a planned spiritual event that has a tremendous effect on the spiritual growth of the souls of the parents and relatives. The parents and relatives will learn many spiritual lessons about love and forgiveness from the event. Whatever the assignments may be, death doesn't occur until the soul's lessons have been completed or a spiritual gift at the soul level has been given. Once the lessons are learned or the gifts are given, the soul returns to heaven in a peaceful state knowing that the spiritual assignment was completed. Death is very similar to a graduation from a university. It's for this reason there will be a great deal of celebration at my funeral. Most of my friends will understand that I have completed a spiritual course at Earth University. Most of my friends will also realize that I will be back again on Earth someday to learn additional lessons.

There are no accidents in life. Death occurs only when the soul's spiritual assignments have been completed.

The experience of death

There are several books on the market today that provide detailed descriptions of the near-death experience. Most of these books have been written by people who have had near calls with death, or who have experienced situations in which their human bodies have died for several minutes and then started functioning again. In both of these near-death situations, the majority of the people involved have reported peaceful, spiritual occurrences. These occurrences, I believe, give us some insight to the transition of the soul from Earth to heaven when actual human death occurs.

No one can tell us exactly when or how we'll experience our deaths. No one can tell us exactly where we'll be when we make our transitions. One thing, however, is becoming obvious to those who are studying near-death cases, and that is, our actual transitions will be very peaceful and painless. This is not surprising considering we have a very merciful God. We may experience human pain and discomfort up to the point of death, but once the dying process starts, it will be filled with love and inner peace. Many now believe that the actual process of dying is a beautiful, exciting experience. Because of the love and tranquillity that is sensed during near-death experiences, many believe that similar feelings of love and peace are sensed as human death occurs.

The events that take place during the first few minutes of a near-death experience are probably very similar to those that occur during the first few minutes of an actual human death. These near-death events are listed below:

Out-of-body sensation: At the time of death, the soul instantaneously removes itself from the human body. In situations in which the human body will experience a great deal of physical pain, such as in a severe car accident, the soul will remove itself just prior to the accident so that the consciousness of the person doesn't experience the pain.

Sense of love and peace: Immediately after leaving the human body, the soul experiences an overwhelming sense of love and peace. There are no sensations of mental or physical pains.

Awareness of death and surroundings: As the soul leaves the human body, it immediately becomes aware that the body is dying. It also becomes aware of the physical surroundings at the place of death.

Begins journey to heaven: The soul senses a dark tunnel with a bright light at the opposite end and starts floating through the tunnel. The soul is fully aware that it's in a different world.

Greeted by friends: At the end of the tunnel, the soul is greeted by beings of light. These beings of light are deceased family members and friends. The reunion is happy and filled with love.

Greeted by Supreme Being: Following the reunion with friends and relatives, the soul is greeted by a Supreme Being of Light. Many of those who have had the near-death experience state that the Supreme Being is Jesus.

Review of life: The Supreme Being leads the soul through a rapid review of its past life on Earth. The soul automatically understands the spiritual significance of every event it has experienced.

The existence of the above seven stages of the near-death experience has been reported to many professional researchers by several hundred people. Not every person reporting the events, however, has experienced all the stages. Some people have only experienced a few of the stages. No one knows for sure whether or not all these stages really exist, or if there are other events that also occur as the soul makes its transition back to heaven. It really doesn't matter how many stages are involved in the transition. What is important is the fact that there is a spiritual afterlife that is filled with peace and love. This spiritual afterlife, which begins at the moment the human body dies, appears to be totally free from physical and mental pain.

Death is a beautiful, exciting experience that opens the door to a spiritual afterlife that is filled with love and peace.

Reincarnation and karma

No one seems to know what really happens to the soul after the Review of Life is completed by the Supreme Being. The religions of the world all present different viewpoints about the afterlife. Most Christians believe that the soul just remains in heaven and lives there for eternity. Some Christians believe that only the souls of believers in Christ stay in heaven after judgement day, while the souls of nonbelievers and sinners are sent to "hell," where they are tormented and punished for eternity. More and more Christians are now believing that the soul returns to Earth in a different human body and lives another life filled with opportunities for learning additional spiritual lessons. This rebirth of the soul is known as reincarnation. Reincarnation is a basic concept in the religions of Hinduism and Buddhism, and is also a common belief among many followers in the New Age movement.

It's quite obvious from the information I have presented in the past few chapters, that I am one of the growing numbers of Christians who believe in reincarnation. The belief in reincarnation has been increasing in the United States during the past three decades. As discussed in an earlier lesson, a 1981 Gallup Poll indicated that 23% of the American adult population now believe in reincarnation. This is about 2% higher than what was found in a similar survey in the early 1960's. An analysis of the 1981 survey results indicated that 25% of the Catholics and 21% of the Protestants now believe in the rebirth of the soul.

A belief in reincarnation doesn't conflict with the basic teachings of Jesus or the belief that we have a loving merciful God. The Christian belief that sinners and nonbelievers will be tormented and punished for eternity in a place called hell is, in my opinion, in direct conflict with the belief that our God is compassionate and merciful. If we truly accept Jesus' teachings that our God is forgiving, does it make sense that God would send nonbelievers and sinners to hell for eternity without another chance to discover the truth? Since God truly loves His children, He wouldn't destroy them because of their human mistakes. A merciful God would give them another chance to learn the truth about the spiritual life. Our God is merciful and compassionate, and reincarnation is His way of giving His children the opportunity to learn the truth.

When people talk about reincarnation, the word karma is often spoken. Karma is a spiritual law which determines the type of life one will have when the soul is reincarnated. Basically the law says that the totality of a person's actions in a successive state of his existence, determines his fate in the next life. What this means is that we all determine the quality of our future lives by the way we live our current lives. If we cause a great deal of pain and suffering during this lifetime, we'll experience a certain amount of pain and suffering in another lifetime. The Law of Karma is similar to the Law of Cause and Effect that we discussed in an earlier lesson. Both of these laws hold us accountable for our daily actions.

Therefore, to guarantee a happy afterlife, we should all live our current lives filled with love and respect for others until the moment our souls make their transitions.

To guarantee a happy afterlife, we should all live our lives filled with love and respect for others until the moment our souls make their transitions.

FOLLOW-UP EXERCISES

(1) Examine the beliefs you have about death and dying. What do you truly believe? Are you scared of dying? Why do you feel the way you do about death?

(2) When you have your *Review of Life* by your Supreme Being, will you be proud of your accomplishments? Is there something you want to change before you go back to heaven? Do you want to tell someone how much you really love them? There is still time to do it.

—PART TWO—

Self-Awareness

"To know thy higher self is to know God"

—Day #8—

Understanding the complex personality

Welcome to Part 2 of this program. This section, called Self-Awareness, has been designed to help you discover hidden aspects about yourself. In the next two lessons, we're going to look at the factors that have influenced the development of your personality and then, through a written inventory, determine which areas in your life require special attention. We're also going to review why many spiritual people believe that you are "perfect" just the way you are. Are you ready to learn more about your distinctive personality?

What is the personality?

Are you aware that you're different from everyone else in this world? Do you realize that there has never been, or will ever be, another person on this planet that thinks, feels, and behaves exactly as you do? It's true. Even if you have a twin, you and your twin have many dissimilar feelings and thoughts. The distinguishing ways you consistently think, feel, and behave is what the psychologists call your personality. The dictionary defines the personality as follows:

Personality — Habitual patterns and qualities of behavior of any individual as expressed by physical and mental activities and attitudes.

The human personality is very complex. In fact, it's so puzzling that psychologists don't understand exactly how it's formed or how it can best be modified. If we understood the personality, there would probably be only one main personality theory in existence. But it isn't that way. There are many theories and many clinical procedures for understanding and treating the personality. In fact, some psychologists have suggested that there are as many theories on the formation and treatment of the personality as there are psychologists.

Early personality theories

There have been many unique personality theories proposed throughout the centuries. In fact, some are quite interesting to review because they are so far-reaching based on today's medical knowledge. Hippocrates, the Greek physician who is now known as the father of medicine, proposed one of the first personality theories around 400 B.C. His theory was that the human personality was determined by the type and quantity of fluid within the body. Hippocrates believed that the body contained four basic types of fluids and that an excess of one or another would produce a certain type of personality. According to Hippocrates, an excess amount of blood caused cheerfulness; an excess of black bile caused depression; an excess of yellow bile caused anger; and an excess of phlegm caused an unemotional behavior. Fortunately for our blood banks, Hippocrates' theory isn't accepted today.

During the next two thousand years, there were very few notable personality theories proposed. Then in 1924, an American psychologist named William Sheldon presented a theory that the personality was determined by a person's body physique. According to Sheldon, the three areas of the body that were important to personality development were the skeleton and muscles, the digestive organs, and the skin and nervous system. Based on Sheldon's research, chubby people were generally more sociable and relaxed; muscular people were generally more aggressive and adventurous; and thin people were generally more self-conscious and hypersensitive. Sheldon's theory isn't accepted today, because psychologists have determined that personalities are not directly related to body physiques.

Of the personality theorists, Sigmund Freud has probably been the most influential. Freud provided us with the first complex and comprehensive personality theory. His theory was the first to stress the importance of the unconscious mind. According to Freud, the personality consists of three interrelated parts—the id, the ego, and the superego. These three parts interacted to determine a person's thoughts, feelings, and actions. Although Freud's personality theory became very popular with the general public a few decades ago, much of his work is now sharply criticized, because it greatly overemphasized the influence of sexual motivations on personality development. Much of Freud's theory is no longer considered valid.

A modern personality theory

Of all the theories that are in existence today, none accurately describe the total functioning of the personality. The human personality is just too complex to be understood. Some theories are still useful, however, because they allow us to examine and predict human behavior patterns under general conditions. One such theory is called the Modified Self Theory. I personally have used this theory several times to examine changes in my own personality. The theory is very straightforward and easy to comprehend once the following definitions are understood.

Self— It's who you really are. It's the human/spiritual being that stands naked in front of the mirror each morning. It's the sum of everything you are. It's your thoughts, beliefs, and feelings. It's your body and soul.

Self-concept— It's who you think you are. It's your perception or image of yourself. It's your honest view of your abilities, appearance, worth, desires, and everything else about you. Although your self-concept is an honest perception, it's often an inaccurate perception.

Ideal self— It's your perception of the "perfect" you. It's what you think you would be if you had no flaws or problems. It's what you dream about becoming, but believe you'll never become.

Aspired self— It's your perception of what you can achieve. It is a level of accomplishment or attainment between the self-concept and the ideal self. It's your image of a reasonable goal.

The Modified Self Theory says that the personality, the way one thinks, feels, and behaves, is determined by how well the experiences in life correspond to one's self-concept and to one's aspired self. If the experiences in life are more abundant or more pleasurable than what a person believes he deserves, then he responds to life in a positive way. On the other hand, if one is not receiving in life what he believes he should, he responds in negative ways.

As an example, a person earning $50,000 a year and living in a $150,000 house may or may not be happy with himself. It depends on his self-concept and his aspired self. If his self-concept, his perception of himself, states that he is only worthy of a $30,000 job and a $90,000 house, and his aspired self says that his goal in life is a $55,000 job and a $160,000 house, chances are he'll be quite pleased with himself, and this will be reflected in a positive personality. On the other hand, if his self-concept is such that he believes that he should be making $75,000 a year and living in a $250,000 house, then he would probably be unhappy with himself, and this would show up in negative actions. This example clearly illustrates that our happiness in life is not directly related to what we have, but is dependent to how well our life experiences correspond to our perceptions of ourselves and our reasonable goals.

Our happiness in life is directly related to how well our life experiences correspond to our perceptions of ourselves and our reasonable goals.

The above statement is one of the keys to happiness, and therefore, is worth repeating. It says that we'll be happy in life if our life experiences correspond to perceptions of ourselves (Self-concept) and our reasonable goals (Aspired self). If there is a significant mismatch, we probably won't be happy. For many of us, there isn't a good match. Nevertheless, we have the opportunity to do one of two things. We can either change our life experiences or change our perceptions of ourselves. This is easier said than done, yet most of us spend a lifetime trying to change one or the other or both.

Factors influencing our self-concepts

By definition, our self-concepts are our images or perceptions of ourselves. They are who we honestly believe we are. Unfortunately, who we believe we are is probably very different from who we really are. Most of us have distorted perceptions about ourselves. Sometimes these distorted perceptions help us in certain life situations, and sometimes they are a hindrance.

Our perceptions about ourselves are the direct result of both nature and nurture. Nature, which is what we inherit, plays a much greater role in the formation of our self-concepts than many of us realize. Recent studies at the University of Minnesota of 68 sets of twins, separated at birth and reunited many years later as adults, have provided some amazing insights into the role of nature on our lives. In one case study it was discovered that a set of male twins separated at birth and reunited at age 39 had led very similar lives.

During separation, both of these male twins had a first wife named Linda, a second wife named Betty, a son named James Alan, and a dog named Toy. They both had also worked as a part-time sheriff, drove the same model car, and had vacationed on the same beach in Florida. It was quite obvious to the researchers at the University that the lives of these two men had been greatly influenced by their genetic makeup. Nature has a major effect on our lives and our self-images.

Nurture, which includes all the environmental factors to which a person is subjected from the time of conception until death, probably has the greatest influence on a person's self-concept. Most psychologists agree that the nurturing that occurs during the first five years of a person's life creates the foundation for most adult perceptions. It's often the relationships between a young child and his immediate family members, particularly the mother, that determines the child's adult personality. A child that grows up in an environment of fear and insecurity will probably become a fearful and insecure adult. A child that is raised by a caring family where love and respect are experienced will most likely grow up to be a caring, loving, and respectful adult.

What type of childhood environment were you exposed to? Was it normal? Was it functional? Was it healthy? It's important to learn what your family environment was during the early years of your life, because that environment has greatly affected (or distorted) your perceptions of yourself and life. Your current self-concept isn't new, but is just a modification of your earliest self-concept. It's unfortunate, but true, that most of us are living our lives today based on misconceptions about ourselves that we developed as children. If our early perceptions of ourselves were of being unlovable and unworthy, then those same perceptions are still part of our self-concepts today. They may have been modified to a certain degree since childhood by significant experiences or professional counseling, but our early perceptions are still with us. The reason why psychologists have written books describing such conditions as the "inner child" and the "child of the past" is to help us understand that the child that we were once is still living within us and is affecting a significant portion of our daily lives.

*It's unfortunate, but true,
that most of us are living our lives
today based on misconceptions about
ourselves that we developed as children.*

The dysfunctional family

It's probably true to say that children raised in an average family today have a somewhat distorted perception of both themselves and life. I say this, because it has been estimated that 96% of the families in the United States are now dysfunctional. This statistic means that the average family is dysfunctional and that 96% of the children in our country may need professional counseling to modify their distorted views of life.

What is a dysfunctional family? It's simply a family that doesn't function well together. It's a family that doesn't provide its members, particularly the children, with a strong sense of well-being. It's a family that is characterized by inconsistency, unpredictability, arbitrary decisions, and chaotic situations. A good example of a dysfunctional family is one in which a parent is an alcoholic or a drug addict. Other examples include families where a parent is a child abuser, a wife beater, or a workaholic. It can even be a family in which a grandparent, a parent, or a child is terminally ill. In a dysfunctional family, the members can't talk openly about their feelings, experiences, and problems. In a dysfunctional family a child must often take on the responsibility of a "missing" parent. In a dysfunctional family the children often live in fear—the fear of abuse, abandonment, being unwanted, being unlovable, and being out of control. Children of dysfunctional families grow up with distorted perceptions of themselves and of life.

Recent studies have shown that children of dysfunctional

families develop specific characteristics, and that these characteristics are often dependent upon the birth order and relative ages of the children. The results of these studies are fascinating and can be used to predict behavior patterns of children. Based on these birth order studies, the following predictions would be made about four children of a dsyfunctional family.

<u>First Born — the "hero" child</u>

- Underlying motivation—a need for approval.

- Characteristics—perfectionist, responsible, mature, reliable, organized, hard working, appears well-adjusted, achiever, conservative, stable, loyal, a "fixer", noble, oversensitive, feelings of inadequacy, egocentric, self-centered.

- Needs—lots of attention, to be the best, to keep everyone happy, to be admired, to be the leader, to justify actions, to make others dependent, to have allies.

- Future employment—company president, doctor, social worker, judge, congressman, teacher.

<u>Second Born — the "rebel" child</u>

- Underlying motivation—a need to belong.

- Characteristics—family scapegoat, gets blamed for everything, rebellious, rejects family, considered a troublemaker, seeks outside involvement, intolerant, uncooperative, vengeful, vindictive, uninvolved, appears maladjusted, gets poor grades, jealous, envious.

- Needs—to belong to a group (any group), to be free, to be his own person, to be different, to prove his usefulness.

- Future employment—motorcycle mechanic, cult leader, rock star, lawyer, writer, reporter.

Third Born —the "lost" child

- Underlying motivation—to be left alone.

- Characteristics—likes isolation, a loner, withdrawn, shy, indecisive, often vacillates, doesn't want responsibility, uninvolved, unable to lead, has difficulty following, procrastinates, impulsive, detached, oblivious to the surroundings, quiet, stays out of trouble.

- Needs—to be alone, to think alone, to ignore things, to have gadgets, to come and go without restrictions, to obtain knowledge, to detach from the family.

- Future employment—production line worker, forest ranger, writer, carpenter, animal trapper, farmer.

Fourth Born —the "mascot" or "clown" child

- Underlying motivation—to be taken seriously.

- Characteristics—sensitive, perceptive, conflict resolver, skilled negotiator, immature, selfish, fearful, often lies, manipulative, demanding, spoiled, impatient, hyperactive, insecure, fragile, emotionally impoverished.

- Needs—to be included, to be listened to, to be secure, to be reassurred.

- Future employment—comedian, contract negotiator, car salesman, musician, actor.

Being a child of a dysfunctional family and having the characteristics that are stated above doesn't mean that you can't be happy in life. In fact, just about all of the happy people in this world fall within one of these categories. The only point that is being made is that we often have certain personality traits that are the direct result of our upbringing in dysfunctional families and, by being aware of these traits, we can take certain actions to overcome them.

If anyone is wondering which group I'm in, let me say that I'm a second born and very much a "rebel" child. Although most of my characteristics and needs are those of the second child, I have also developed some first born qualities, because of a unique situation that existed within my childhood family during the early years of my life. Unique family situations and abnormal parent/child relationships are very common and, therefore, there are many exceptions to the personality predictions that are based on birth order.

In my own family today there is just one child, and he is definitely a "hero" child. My 19 year old son, who by the age of 17 was an Eagle Scout, a Dale Carnegie Course graduate, and a DCC graduate assistant, has the characteristics and needs that are expected from a first born of a dysfunctional family. The dysfunctionality of my own early family had nothing to do with alcohol or drugs, but was the result of my inability to create and maintain a nurturing family environment during the years my first wife was emotionally depressed and the years that followed her tragic death. My son, who was only two years old when his mother died, was greatly influenced by his early environment.

How to develop a healthy self-concept

Developing a healthy self-concept is an important step in creating a happier life. This isn't an easy task, however, and will probably take a fair amount of time to complete. But in this case, doing the task is just as enjoyable as completing the task. There are many ways of forming positive self-images, and each one of us must decide for ourselves which steps should be taken first. In my opinion, any of the following activities would be a good start.

- *Getting involved in a personal support group:* Have a weekly meeting with 3 or 4 compatible friends for the purpose of discussing and supporting each others' personal goals and desires.

- *Attending local recovery programs:* There are many excellent programs available to assist you in recovery such as Alcoholics Anonymous, Al-Anon, Alateen, Adult Children of Alcoholics,

Narcotics Anonymous, Codependents Anonymous, Gamblers Anonymous, Gam-Anon, Emotions Anonymous, Smokers Anonymous, and Agoraphobics in Motion.

- *Going to church:* The services and sermons must be uplifting and meaningful. They shouldn't make you feel like a sinner.

- *Taking time to meditate and pray:* It's beneficial to set aside 30 minutes a day for this life-changing step.

- *Reading spiritual and self-help books:* There are many books in the library that can change your life.

- *Volunteering for charity work:* Most of the charities are looking for free help, and the more you give, the more you'll get in return.

- *Taking human relations classes:* The Dale Carnegie Course is an excellent personal development program and a great way to meet new people.

- *Developing an image board or book:* Paste pictures on a poster board or in a book that represent your goals and aspirations.

- *Keeping a journal of positive thoughts and experiences:* It's nice to recall positive thoughts and achievements on days that are less than positive.

- *Attending a spiritual retreat center for a weekend or longer:* Many churches sponsor monthly and annual retreats.

These activities really work. I have done them all except attend a local recovery program. Those who regularly attend the recovery programs, however, tell me that their lives have greatly improved since becoming involved. Which steps are you ready to take?

The "Perfect" personality theory

The "Perfect" Personality Theory is not perfect, it's only called perfect. It's called that, because it's based on the spiritual Law of Perfection which says:

Everything in God's universe is perfect just the way it is.

The foundation for this theory is found in two of the spiritual concepts we developed in earlier lessons. These concepts are:

- You are the creator of your own unique divine plan. You are also your own creation that is living out this plan. You designed every important aspect of your life on Earth. You selected your parents and determined your childhood experiences before you were born.

- Your real purpose in life is to correct minor imperfections in your soul. By living within your divine plan, these imperfections will be corrected and you'll experience a closer "oneness" with God.

The Perfect Personality Theory says: Since everything in God's universe is perfect, our current personalities must also be perfect. Our personalities must have been precisely and flawlessly developed during our earthly activities in accordance with our divine plans. It's by changing our personalities so that they are more in tune with spiritual teachings (love, respect, harmony, forgiveness, etc.) that we fulfill our divine purposes and correct the minor imperfections in our souls. It's through our human responses to human situations that our spiritual souls grow.

By changing our personalities so that they are more in tune with spiritual teachings, we fulfill our divine purposes and correct the minor imperfections in our souls.

FOLLOW-UP EXERCISES

(1) Complete the self-evaluation sheets on the following four pages. Do you think your friends would agree with the perceptions you have of yourself? If possible, share your perceptions with a close friend.

(2) Think about the significant people in your childhood who influenced your early self-concept. Were these people loving, caring, and understanding? Did you feel safe and secure with them? Were you able to talk to them about your feelings and thoughts? Did you really have a chance to develop a healthy self-concept?

"SELF PERCEPTION" WORK SHEET

Directions: Write down your perceptions of yourself.

SELF-CONCEPT *(This is my perception of the "real" me.)*

IDEAL SELF

(This is my perception of the "perfect" me.)

ASPIRED SELF

(This is my perception of the "potential" me.)

ASPIRATIONS vs ACCOMPLISHMENTS

WORK SHEET

Objective: To determine which areas in your life need additional attention by comparing accomplishment scores to aspiration scores.

Directions: In the first column, give yourself up to 10 points according to the importance of that aspiration or goal to you. In the second column, evaluate how well you are presently doing in attaining that goal, and give yourself a score up to the amount you gave yourself in the first column. In the third column, enter the difference between your aspiration score and your accomplishment score. Circle the self-concept statements that have the highest "difference" scores. These statements should represent areas in your life that are causing you dissatisfaction.

	Aspiration score	Accomplish- ment score	Difference score

Social self-concepts

I'm always friendly to people.

I'm fun to be with.

I enjoy being at parties.

I can be trusted with secrets.

I have many old and new friends.

(add your own)——

(add your own)——

Total

Personal self-concepts

I'm a very honest person.

I take good care of my body.

I'm in control of my drinking.

My overall appearance is good.

I am free of drugs.

(add your own)——

(add your own)——

Total

ASPIRATIONS vs ACCOMPLISHMENTS

WORK SHEET

	Aspiration score	Accomplish-ment score	Difference score
Family self-concepts			
I'm a loving member of my family.	___	___	___
I enjoy my role in the family.	___	___	___
I spend time with each family member.	___	___	___
I do my share of the family chores.	___	___	___
Family closeness is important to me.	___	___	___
(add your own)——	___	___	___
(add your own)——	___	___	___
Total	___	___	___

Spiritual self-concepts
I understand my spiritual nature.
I'm active in church affairs.
I pray and meditate regularly.
I help others grow spiritually.
I am a loving child of God.
(add your own)——
(add your own)——

Total

Work self-concepts
I'm a good, honest worker.
I'm loyal to my boss.
I'm a team player.
I'm optimistic about my future career.
I enjoy my work.
(add your own)——
(add your own)——

Total

ASPIRATIONS vs ACCOMPLISHMENTS

WORK SHEET

Educational self-concepts	Aspiration score	Accomplish-ment score	Difference score
I'm knowledgeable about current affairs.	___	___	___
I take time to read good books.	___	___	___
I watch educational TV programs.	___	___	___
I'm proud of my commitment to learn.	___	___	___
I'm proud of my educational achievements.	___	___	___
(add your own)—	___	___	___
(add your own)—	___	___	___
Total	___	___	___

Recreational self-concepts

I take time to do the things I enjoy.
I take relaxing vacations.
I enjoy being involved in new activities.
I often help others enjoy life.
I believe in having fun.
(add your own)——
(add your own)——

Total

Sexual self-concepts

I have a healthy attitude about sex.
I maintain a sexy body.
I'm a tender, caring partner.
I practice safe sex.
I'm proud of my performance.
(add your own)——
(add your own)——

Total

—Day #9—

Conducting a personal inventory

In bold red letters the sign in the front window of the store said:

-CLOSED FOR INVENTORY-

I used to wonder why a high volume department store would close its doors to its customers in the middle of the week for one full day just to take an inventory of stock. And they would do it four times a year. In my mind, this wasn't rational. Was taking an inventory that important? Couldn't they do it at night after closing?

So I talked to the manager of the store one day, and he explained it to me. He said, "Years ago we used to conduct our inventories just once a year, but what we found during those years was that we wasted a lot of time and energy between annual inventories just rearranging items we couldn't sell. Our stockroom shelves became so cluttered with unsaleable items that we didn't have any room to stock items we could sell. Between inventories we never really knew which stock items were important for the growth of our company. Now, however, because we conduct four thorough inventories a year, we know exactly which items are important for maintaining a prosperous business. Those items that aren't important, we sell at discount prices or give them away to charities. In the long run, our business is much more efficient now, and our annual profits are much greater. Taking the inventory process seriously has really helped us to understand our business."

Wouldn't it be great if we could use the same inventory process to help us understand ourselves better? Can you imagine how much easier our lives would be, if we could honestly examine them and determine which items are no longer important for our happiness and growth, and then discard those items? Well we can conduct inventories of our lives. It's very difficult, but we can. The difficulty is mainly because our fears and insecurities won't allow us to be completely honest with ourselves.

Conducting an in-depth inventory of the "self" is fairly laborious. Often it takes days and sometimes even weeks to complete. A few years ago while attending a 28-day spiritual retreat center, I spent four days writing an inventory of my life. There must have been a thousand questions on the inventory sheets. They covered every aspect of my life including relationships, activities, thoughts, and beliefs. Through that inventory I was able to see how my original personality was developed and then modified over the years. When I closely examined my interactions with my parents, siblings, spouses, son, and other significant people, I was able to uncover several character defects hidden deep within me. These character defects were interfering with my relationships and beliefs. Taking an inventory of my life was one of the best things I ever did for myself.

Are you ready to take an inventory of your life? Millions of people across our country will take one this year, because it's the fourth step of the famous Twelve-Step Program. This is the program that many self-help groups are now using to help people recover from addictions and personality disorders. Many self-help organizations now believe that taking an inventory is one of the most important steps in developing a thorough understanding of oneself.

FOLLOW-UP EXERCISES

(1) Complete the *Inventory Work Sheets* on the following pages. Get in touch with your deepest feelings about each person in the inventory. This exercise is the most difficult part of this transformation program. Ask God to help you with this task.

(2) Make a list of the people you need to forgive. Also make a list of the people you would like forgiveness from. Review this list tomorrow after you read the lesson on forgiveness.

INVENTORY WORK SHEET

Relationship with: *MOTHER / STEPMOTHER*

Directions: Please answer the following questions as honestly as possible. How you answer the last five questions indicates whether or not you need to work on your relationship with your mother.

EARLY MEMORIES

	Disagree			Agree	
1. My memories of my mother are happy ones.	O	O	O	O	O
2. My mother was a kind, loving person.	O	O	O	O	O
3. My mother protected me when I needed protection.	O	O	O	O	O
4. My mother taught me the importance of love.	O	O	O	O	O
5. My mother often told me she loved me.	O	O	O	O	O
6. Often my mother and I spent quality times together.	O	O	O	O	O
7. My mother disciplined me fairly.	O	O	O	O	O
8. I could always count on my mother.	O	O	O	O	O
9. My mother was proud of me.	O	O	O	O	O

10. My mother would take time to listen to me.	O	O	O	O	O
11. My mother wouldn't embarrass me.	O	O	O	O	O
12. My mother would often hold me.	O	O	O	O	O
13. My mother never made sexual advances towards me.	O	O	O	O	O
14. My mother tried to be a good mother.	O	O	O	O	O
15. My mother encouraged me to set high standards.	O	O	O	O	O
16. My mother took interest in my achievements.	O	O	O	O	O
17. My mother supported me in my goals.	O	O	O	O	O
18. I was always proud to be with my mother.	O	O	O	O	O
19. I could be truthful with my mother.	O	O	O	O	O
20. My mother's anger was normal in my opinion.	O	O	O	O	O

CURRENT THOUGHTS

21. I don't blame my mother for my current problems.	O	O	O	O	O
22. I have no guilty feelings concerning my mother.	O	O	O	O	O
23. My mother showed me she loved me in her own way.	O	O	O	O	O
24. I love my mother deeply, and I have told her so.	O	O	O	O	O
25. I totally accept my relationship with my mother.	O	O	O	O	O

INVENTORY WORK SHEET

Relationship with: _FATHER / STEPFATHER_

Directions: Please answer the following questions as honestly as possible. How you answer the last five questions indicates whether or not you need to work on your relationship with your father.

EARLY MEMORIES

	Disagree		Agree	
1. My memories of my father are happy ones.	O	O	O	O
2. My father was a kind, loving person.	O	O	O	O
3. My father protected me when I needed protection.	O	O	O	O
4. My father taught me the importance of love.	O	O	O	O
5. My father often told me he loved me.	O	O	O	O
6. Often my father and I spent quality times together.	O	O	O	O
7. My father disciplined me fairly.	O	O	O	O
8. I could always count on my father.	O	O	O	O
9. My father was proud of me.	O	O	O	O

O O O O O O O O O O   O O O O O

O O O O O O O O O O   O O O O O

O O O O O O O O O O   O O O O O

O O O O O O O O O O   O O O O O

O O O O O O O O O O   O O O O O

10. My father would take time to listen to me.
11. My father wouldn't embarrass me.
12. My father would often hold me.
13. My father never made sexual advances towards me.
14. My father tried to be a good father.
15. My father encouraged me to set high standards.
16. My father took interest in my achievements.
17. My father supported me in my goals.
18. I was always proud to be with my father.
19. I could be truthful with my father.
20. My father's anger was normal in my opinion.

CURRENT THOUGHTS

21. I don't blame my father for my current problems.
22. I have no guilty feelings concerning my father.
23. My father showed me he loved me in his own way.
24. I love my father deeply, and I have told him so.
25. I totally accept my relationship with my father.

INVENTORY WORK SHEET

Relationship with: *SISTER*

Directions: Please answer the following questions as honestly as possible. How you answer the last five questions indicates whether or not you need to work on your relationship with your sister.

EARLY MEMORIES

	Disagree			Agree	
1. My memories of my sister are happy ones.	O	O	O	O	O
2. My sister was a kind, loving person.	O	O	O	O	O
3. My sister protected me when I needed protection.	O	O	O	O	O
4. My sister taught me the importance of love.	O	O	O	O	O
5. My sister often told me she loved me.	O	O	O	O	O
6. Often my sister and I spent quality times together.	O	O	O	O	O
7. My sister and I were close.	O	O	O	O	O
8. I could always count on my sister.	O	O	O	O	O
9. My sister was proud of me.	O	O	O	O	O

10. My sister would take time to listen to me. ○ ○ ○ ○ ○

11. My sister wouldn't embarrass me. ○ ○ ○ ○ ○

12. My sister would often hold me. ○ ○ ○ ○ ○

13. My sister never made sexual advances towards me. ○ ○ ○ ○ ○

14. My sister tried to be a good sister. ○ ○ ○ ○ ○

15. My sister encouraged me to set high standards. ○ ○ ○ ○ ○

16. My sister took interest in my achievements. ○ ○ ○ ○ ○

17. My sister supported me in my goals. ○ ○ ○ ○ ○

18. I was always proud to be with my sister. ○ ○ ○ ○ ○

19. I could be truthful with my sister. ○ ○ ○ ○ ○

20. My sister's anger was normal in my opinion. ○ ○ ○ ○ ○

CURRENT THOUGHTS

21. I don't blame my sister for my current problems. ○ ○ ○ ○ ○

22. I have no guilty feelings concerning my sister. ○ ○ ○ ○ ○

23. My sister showed me she loved me in her own way. ○ ○ ○ ○ ○

24. I love my sister deeply, and I have told her so. ○ ○ ○ ○ ○

25. I totally accept my relationship with my sister. ○ ○ ○ ○ ○

INVENTORY WORK SHEET

Relationship with: _BROTHER_

Directions: Please answer the following questions as honestly as possible. How you answer the last five questions indicates whether or not you need to work on your relationship with your brother.

EARLY MEMORIES

	Disagree			Agree
1. My memories of my brother are happy ones.	O	O	O	O
2. My brother was a kind, loving person.	O	O	O	O
3. My brother protected me when I needed protection.	O	O	O	O
4. My brother taught me the importance of love.	O	O	O	O
5. My brother often told me he loved me.	O	O	O	O
6. Often my brother and I spent quality times together.	O	O	O	O
7. My brother and I were good friends.	O	O	O	O
8. I could always count on my brother.	O	O	O	O
9. My brother was proud of me.	O	O	O	O

10. My brother would take time to listen to me. ○ ○ ○ ○ ○
11. My brother wouldn't embarrass me. ○ ○ ○ ○ ○
12. My brother would often hold me. ○ ○ ○ ○ ○
13. My brother never made sexual advances towards me. ○ ○ ○ ○ ○
14. My brother tried to be a good brother. ○ ○ ○ ○ ○
15. My brother encouraged me to set high standards. ○ ○ ○ ○ ○
16. My brother took interest in my achievements. ○ ○ ○ ○ ○
17. My brother supported me in my goals. ○ ○ ○ ○ ○
18. I was always proud to be with my brother. ○ ○ ○ ○ ○
19. I could be truthful with my brother. ○ ○ ○ ○ ○
20. My brother's anger was normal in my opinion. ○ ○ ○ ○ ○

CURRENT THOUGHTS

21. I don't blame my brother for my current problems. ○ ○ ○ ○ ○
22. I have no guilty feelings concerning my brother. ○ ○ ○ ○ ○
23. My brother showed me he loved me in his own way. ○ ○ ○ ○ ○
24. I love my brother deeply, and I have told him so. ○ ○ ○ ○ ○
25. I totally accept my relationship with my brother. ○ ○ ○ ○ ○

INVENTORY WORK SHEET

Relationship with: *SPOUSE / SIGNIFICANT OTHER*

Directions: Please answer the following questions as honestly as possible. How you answer the last five questions indicates whether or not you need to work on your relationship with this significant person.

EARLY MEMORIES

	Disagree			Agree	
1. My memories of this person are happy ones.	○	○	○	○	○
2. This person was kind and loving.	○	○	○	○	○
3. This person protected me when I needed protection.	○	○	○	○	○
4. This person taught me the importance of love.	○	○	○	○	○
5. This person and I respected each other.	○	○	○	○	○
6. This person and I spent quality times together.	○	○	○	○	○
7. This person never cheated on me.	○	○	○	○	○
8. I could always count on this person.	○	○	○	○	○
9. This person was proud of me.	○	○	○	○	○

o o o o o o o o o o o   o o o o o

o o o o o o o o o o   o o o o o

o o o o o o o o o o o   o o o o o

o o o o o o o o o o o   o o o o o

o o o o o o o o o o o   o o o o o

10. This person would take time to listen to me.
11. This person wouldn't embarrass me.
12. This person would often hold me.
13. This person and I had a healthy sexual relationship.
14. This person was my best friend.
15. This person encouraged me to set high standards.
16. This person took interest in my achievements.
17. This person supported me in my goals.
18. I was always proud to be with this person.
19. I could be truthful with this person.
20. This person's anger was normal in my opinion.

CURRENT THOUGHTS

21. I don't blame this person for my current problems.
22. I have no guilty feelings concerning this person.
23. The love we shared was a very special love.
24. My love for this person will live forever.
25. I totally accept my relationship with this person.

INVENTORY WORK SHEET

Relationship with: *A CHILD*

Directions: Please answer the following questions as honestly as possible. How you answer the last five questions indicates whether or not you need to work on your relationship with this child.

EARLY MEMORIES

	Disagree		Agree	
1. My memories of this child are happy ones.	O	O	O	O
2. This child was kind and loving.	O	O	O	O
3. This child brought me great joy and happiness.	O	O	O	O
4. This child taught me the importance of loving.	O	O	O	O
5. This child and I respected each other.	O	O	O	O
6. This child and I spent quality times together.	O	O	O	O
7. I was able to give this child freedom to grow.	O	O	O	O
8. I could always count on this child.	O	O	O	O
9. This child was proud of me.	O	O	O	O

○ ○ ○ ○ ○ ○ ○ ○ ○ ○   ○ ○ ○ ○ ○

○ ○ ○ ○ ○ ○ ○ ○ ○ ○   ○ ○ ○ ○ ○

○ ○ ○ ○ ○ ○ ○ ○ ○ ○   ○ ○ ○ ○ ○

○ ○ ○ ○ ○ ○ ○ ○ ○ ○   ○ ○ ○ ○ ○

○ ○ ○ ○ ○ ○ ○ ○ ○ ○   ○ ○ ○ ○ ○

10. This child would take time to listen to me.
11. This child wouldn't embarrass me.
12. This child and I would often hold each other.
13. This child and I had a healthy relationship.
14. This child and I would share our dreams.
15. This child encouraged me to set high standards.
16. This child took interest in my achievements.
17. This child supported me in my goals.
18. I was always proud to be with this child.
19. I could be truthful with this child.
20. This child and I were happy together.

CURRENT THOUGHTS

21. I don't blame this child for my current problems.
22. I have no guilty feelings concerning this child.
23. The love we shared was a very special love.
24. My love for this child will live forever.
25. I totally accept my relationship with this child.

INVENTORY WORK SHEET

Relationship with: A SIGNIFICANT PERSON

Directions: Please answer the following questions as honestly as possible. How you answer the last five questions indicates whether or not you need to work on your relationship with this significant person.

EARLY MEMORIES

	Disagree				Agree
1. My memories of this person are happy ones.	O	O	O	O	O
2. This person was kind and loving.	O	O	O	O	O
3. This person protected me when I needed protection.	O	O	O	O	O
4. This person taught me the importance of love.	O	O	O	O	O
5. This person and I respected each other.	O	O	O	O	O
6. This person and I spent quality times together.	O	O	O	O	O
7. This person never harmed me.	O	O	O	O	O
8. I could always count on this person.	O	O	O	O	O
9. This person was proud of me.	O	O	O	O	O

o o o o o o o o o o o   o o o o o

o o o o o o o o o o o   o o o o o

o o o o o o o o o o o   o o o o o

o o o o o o o o o o o   o o o o o

o o o o o o o o o o o   o o o o o

10. This person would take time to listen to me.
11. This person wouldn't embarrass me.
12. This person would often hold me.
13. This person and I had a healthy sexual relationship.
14. This person made me feel worthy.
15. This person encouraged me to set high standards.
16. This person took interest in my achievements.
17. This person supported me in my goals.
18. I was always proud to be with this person.
19. I could be truthful with this person.
20. This person's anger was normal in my opinion.

CURRENT THOUGHTS

21. I don't blame this person for my current problems.
22. I have no guilty feelings concerning this person.
23. This person shows me love in a special way.
24. I have a deep love for this person.
25. I totally accept my relationship with this person.

INVENTORY WORK SHEET

Directions: Please answer the following questions about *FEAR* as honestly as possible. Try to see how past experiences have influenced your behavior.

1. Are you scared of new situations in life? Do you fear going to new places and meeting new people? Explain:

2. In what ways do you feel inadequate? Explain:

3. Are you oversensitive to comments made about you, your family, and your ideas? Explain:

4. Are you impatient? Do you often have a restless eagerness to do something or go somewhere? Do you feel annoyance when delays occur? Explain:

5. Are you jealous of people? Do you envy what they have? Explain:

6. Do you have a tendency to reject new ideas and beliefs? Does it make you feel uncomfortable to hear people talk about goals in life? Explain:

INVENTORY WORK SHEET

Directions: Please answer the following questions about *INSECURITY* as honestly as possible. Try to see how past experiences have influenced your behavior.

1.   Do you have a tendency to procrastinate? Do you put off doing something unpleasant until a future time?
Explain:

2.   Do you have a dependency on other people? Explain:

3.   Do you often worry about things that are not important? Do you feel troubled and uneasy about the future?
Explain:

4. Do you have difficulty sleeping at night because of daily problems? Explain:

5. Do you have problems making decisions about what to buy and where to go? Explain:

6. Are you able to tell others exactly what you think and feel? Explain:

INVENTORY WORK SHEET

Directions: Please answer the following questions about *SOLITUDE* as honestly as possible. Try to see how past experiences have influenced your behavior.

1. Do you have a tendency to isolate yourself at family gatherings? Explain:

2. Do you avoid joining clubs and social functions? Explain:

3. Are you filled with self-pity? How often do you feel sorry for yourself? Explain:

4. Do you feel that people don't understand you or respect you for what you are? Explain:

5. Are you a victim of circumstances? Do you feel that only bad things happen to you? Explain:

6. Do you dress or act differently so that other people will stay away from you? Explain:

INVENTORY WORK SHEET

Directions: Please answer the following questions about *FUTILITY* as honestly as possible. Try to see how past experiences have influenced your behavior.

1. Are you a perfectionist? Are your standards much higher than normal? Explain:

2. Do you believe that every job that you do must be done well? Is the obtainment of high marks in all areas of your life important to you? Explain:

3. Do you have a lot of false pride? Do you have problems admitting your human weaknesses? Explain:

4. Do you have a grandiose attitude? Are you often trying to seem more important than others. Explain:

5. Do you have excessive spiritual pride? Do you think that God or Spirit is working mainly through you? Explain:

6. Do you feel guilty that you have not reached the high goals you have set for your life? Do you often feel like a failure? Explain:

INVENTORY WORK SHEET

Directions: Please answer the following questions about *ANGER* as honestly as possible. Try to see how past experiences have influenced your behavior.

1. Do you blame others for your current problems in life? Explain:

2. Do you act violently towards people you love? Explain:

3. Do you find it difficult to tolerate many situations in life? Do you often interfere in the lives of others? Explain:

4. Do you often rationalize your actions? Are you often explaining your position about situations? Explain:

5. Are you filled with vengeance? Do you believe that an injury should be returned for an injury? Explain:

6. Are you often manipulating people to your way of thinking? Explain:

INVENTORY WORK SHEET

Directions: Please answer the following questions about *GUILT* as honestly as possible. Try to see how past experiences have influenced your behavior.

1.   Do you feel abnormally guilty about the things you have done in life? Explain:

2.   Are you often dishonest about situations to cover a guilty feeling? Do you lie a great deal? Explain:

3.   Do you believe that you should be punished for many of the things you have done in life? Explain:

4. Do you often establish alibis for the activities you've been involved with? Explain:

5. Are you often justifying your position on a subject, because you feel guilty about your thoughts? Explain:

6. Do you feel guilty about not having better control over your life? Explain:

INVENTORY WORK SHEET

Directions: Please answer the following questions about *YOURSELF* as honestly as possible. Try to see how past experiences have influenced your behavior.

1. Do your friends see you as a loving person? Are they aware of your deep feelings? Explain:

2. Do you feel a great deal of inner security? Do you understand that you are loved and protected at all times? Explain:

3. Are you at peace with yourself? Is there an absence of mental conflict in your life? Explain:

4. Do you accept the relationships and situations in your life? Do you look forward to new adventures with a positive attitude? Explain:

5. Are all of your relationships fulfilling? Do you always see the best in people? Explain:

6. Are you happy? Are you happy knowing that life is beautiful and exciting? Are you happy knowing that you're growing right now as you complete this last question of this inventory? Explain:

—PART THREE—

Practical Applications of Spiritual Knowledge

"𝕎𝕚𝕤𝕕𝕠𝕞 𝕚𝕤 𝕊𝕡𝕚𝕣𝕚𝕥𝕦𝕒𝕝 𝕜𝕟𝕠𝕨𝕝𝕖𝕕𝕘𝕖 𝕚𝕟 𝕒𝕔𝕥𝕚𝕠𝕟"

—Day #10—

Freeing the mind through forgiveness

Welcome to Part 3 of this program. In this section, called *Practical Applications of Spiritual Knowledge,* we're going to examine ways in which you can greatly enhance the quality of your daily life. We're going to address such things as forgiveness, self-esteem, inner peace, meditation, and positive attitudes. Are you ready to make some major changes in your life? This section of the program has been specifically designed to help you do just that.

The need to forgive

Two years ago, I gave a series of talks called *"Tomorrow's Dreams Begin Today."* The talks were very uplifting and promoted the idea that all personal dreams can come true if the dreams don't interfere with anyone's divine plan, and if the proper spiritual and practical steps are taken. Following the second session, a lady named Judy approached me and told me that she didn't believe in dreaming. She said that dreaming of future events was only for innocent children. I was very interested in hearing her ideas, so we sat down and discussed her thoughts about dreaming.

As we talked, Judy expressed a great deal of negativity about several situations that were occurring in her life. She told me her husband had walked out on her a year earlier and had recently filed for a divorce. She told me her children really didn't like her anymore, because of the lies her husband had told them about her.

She said she had a job as a waitress, but was probably going to get fired, because several customers had complained about her negative attitude. She continued to tell me story after story about how she was being rejected by many of her friends and relatives. She said she had often thought about ending her life, but wasn't able to do it. She told me if she did commit suicide, it would teach her mother a lesson. When I heard that comment, it became clear to me that Judy had a much more serious problem than just the ones about dreaming and getting along with people.

Judy wanted to talk about her problems and, since I had the time, I was willing to listen. After talking for about ten minutes, she started to cry. She cried for a few minutes and then got very angry. With a great deal of hostility in her voice, she said, "I want to tell you what my mother did to me when I was four years old. She rejected me. I'll never forgive her for giving me away to a stranger to raise. She gave me away and then left home. Six months later she married a man in the army, and I haven't seen her since." I asked her what had happened to her father, and she told me that he was killed in a car accident when she was three years old. I asked her how she felt about her father, and she answered exactly the way I thought she would. She told me she couldn't forgive him either for leaving her.

It was becoming quite obvious to me that her feelings of being rejected by so many people in her current life were the direct result of the rejection she experienced when both her mother and father left her as a child. Judy never completely understood or accepted those feelings. Because of the fears and insecurities she developed in her early childhood, she was constantly overreacting to situations in her current life that she perceived as abandonment. Judy was a very unhappy person and was continuously destroying the relationships she developed in life.

If Judy is to become a happy person, one of the first things she must do is recognize the anxieties she has concerning her childhood rejections, and then forgive everyone involved. Attending spiritual classes and reading positive thinking books may help her to a limited degree, but because of the instability of her personality, the chances of her becoming very happy in life without first addressing her deep-seated feelings of rejection are slim. Somehow, the anger and fears associated with the childhood rejections must be eliminated before she can start building a new life.

There are three paths Judy can travel to resolve her childhood issues. The first is through years of psychological counseling; the second is through months of spiritual counseling; and the third is a combination of both. Because we are Spiritual Beings and have a compassionate God, I always recommend that spiritual counseling be the major part of any therapy for resolving issues that cause unhappiness. Once Judy can understand and accept the spiritual significance of her childhood experiences and perceive them as opportunities to learn about unconditional love and forgiveness, she'll become a much happier person. Judy has a great opportunity to learn spiritual lessons. The longer she resists the lessons, however, the more intense the mental and physical pains in her life will become.

Judy's story isn't that uncommon. Most of us are living our lives with unresolved issues from the past. The deep-seated negative emotions we have as a result of not addressing these issues, cause us to act in the unloving ways many of us do today. Because most of us haven't taken the time to understand and forgive our parents and others for harmful childhood events, we continue to live our lives with fears and insecurities. The key to resolving many unforgivable events is an awareness that the people who did us harm were doing the best they could at the time of the event. Once we understand this, it becomes easier to forgive and forget. Without true forgiveness, however, the negative feelings that resulted from earlier events will continue to bring unhappiness into our lives. If we're to live happier lives, we must be willing to forgive everyone, including God and ourselves, for past harmful events.

If we're to live happier lives, we must be willing to forgive everyone, including God and ourselves, for past harmful events.

Main reason for forgiving

This past summer I watched one of God's natural miracles occur in my own backyard. It was the transformation of a caterpillar into a butterfly. I didn't see every step of the metamorphosis, but I did observe three of the stages. I watched as one caterpillar formed its pupa. I observed a physical transformation within another pupa. And I saw a butterfly emerging from a similar pupa. As I observed the newly transformed butterfly breaking out of its pupa, I became aware that it was having difficulty becoming free. A portion of the butterfly's body seemed to be stuck to its cocoon. The butterfly was unable to break loose and fly away. As I sat there, I wondered if the butterfly would ever free itself and enjoy the life it was created to experience. It never did. It died without ever experiencing flight.

I tell you this story about the dying butterfly, because there is a great lesson to be learned from its sad ending. The butterfly got stuck in one of its stages of transformation. It had made many miraculous changes in its life, and had successfully grown from an egg to a caterpillar to a pupa to a butterfly. But as soon as it became a butterfly, it died without experiencing the glory of being a butterfly. It died prematurely, because it couldn't free itself from a past stage of life. How many of us have made miraculous changes in our lives, but emotionally died somewhere along the way, because we were unable to free ourselves from the past events in our lives? How many of us have never been able to get off the ground and fly, because we have held on to the emotional pains of the past? How many of us are emotionally dying daily, because we can't forgive the people who injured us during our childhoods? The truth is, most of us can't easily forgive, because our egos are in control of our lives. Until we truly forgive everyone who has harmed us, we'll never experience the glory that we were designed to experience.

The main reason for forgiving is to bring freedom and peace of mind to the individuals involved in a harmful event, so they can move on with their lives. The person who benefits the most from the act of forgiveness is the forgiver. It's the forgiver, not the one who is being forgiven, who really feels the emotional freedom from the past. The forgiver is like the emerging butterfly that finally breaks loose from its pupa and flies away. It never again feels the entrapment and control from its earlier life. The forgiver, like the butterfly, becomes free to experience life to its fullest.

There have been many events in my life that have proven to me that the act of forgiveness is mostly for the forgiver and not for the one being forgiven. For 14 years of my life, I couldn't forgive my first wife for committing suicide. I allowed her act of suicide to distort my views of life and to interfere with my daily living. I was unwilling to forgive her for "rejecting" me, and at the same time, creating within me a tremendous guilt. I also held her responsible for all the difficulties I had during the immediate years that followed her death. My unwillingness to let go of the past did me a great deal of harm. My unwillingness to forgive her, however, was not causing her any problems, since she had already made her transition back to heaven. Until the day I finally forgave her, which was 14 years after the suicide, my life was filled with deep guilt, anger, and resentment. It didn't always show, but it was always there. There were very few days during those 14 years that I didn't think about her and her suicide. The event had control over my life. I needed to forgive her. But I needed to do it for me, not for her. When I finally did forgive her, my life completely changed. It wasn't until that day of forgiveness that I became free to move on with my life.

---

*The main reason for forgiving
is to bring freedom and
peace of mind to the <u>forgiver.</u>*

Spiritual aspects of forgiveness

The stories about Judy's difficult childhood and the dying butterfly are told to illustrate the fact that forgiveness is a very important and practical step toward happiness. Forgiveness is a requirement if the mind is to be free of the negative emotions that were generated during past experiences. If we can't forgive, our lives become controlled by our perceptions of past events. Although the act of forgiveness is a practical way of liberating the mind, it's also a very spiritual occurrence. Forgiveness is a way of experiencing love, and the experience of love is the main reason we're living on Earth.

Jesus was constantly talking about love and forgiveness when He was living among us. He told us that the two most important commandments to obey were the ones about love. In Matthew 22: 37-39, Jesus said,

Love the Lord your God with all your heart and with all your soul and with all your mind. This is the first and greatest commandment. And the second is like it: Love your neighbor as yourself.

Jesus was telling us we should have an enormous amount of love for God, for ourselves, and for others. We have also been told about the importance of love from other sources. The people who have had near-death experiences have reported back to us that based on their spiritual events, love is the most important aspect of life. The importance of feeling love and allowing it to flow from us to others can't be overstated. When we're unwilling to forgive someone for an act that has harmed us, we're blocking this natural flow of love. The act of forgiveness is a spiritual event that reopens the natural channels of love between us and everything else.

The spiritual Law of Cause and Effect clearly indicates what will happen if we don't forgive. According to this law, if we don't forgive others, others won't forgive us. On the other hand, if we live a life filled with forgiveness, others will always forgive us. Most of us have experienced the consequences of this law. Isn't it much easier to forgive someone who has a forgiving nature, than to forgive someone who carries grudges and resentments for others? The Bible supports this law when it says in Luke 6:37,38:

Forgive, and you will be forgiven—For the measure you give will be the measure you get back.

Jesus also emphasized the importance of forgiveness when He told us how to pray. There are many passages in the Bible that tell us that "believing" and "forgiving" are the two key actions that must first occur if our prayers are to come true. In Mark 11:24,25, Jesus said,

You can pray for anything, and if you believe, you can have it: it's yours! But when you are praying, first forgive anyone you are holding a grudge against, so that your Father in heaven will forgive you of your sins too.

I believe the reason so many wonderful things have happened to me during the past five years is because I have discovered for myself the power of belief and the magic of forgiveness. During the past five years, I haven't had any significant ill feelings towards anyone. Because of this, I have been free to experience life to its fullest.

The act of forgiveness is a spiritual event that reopens the natural channels of love between us and everything else.

How to forgive

There are many good books in the library that teach us how to do things. By reading these books, we can learn how to build furniture, repair cars, paint pictures, and do many other physical tasks. These books are very useful, because they help our rational minds to understand the logical mechanics of creating physical objects. Our intellectual minds greatly benefit from these "how to" books. The subject of how to forgive isn't normally discussed in books. This is because the act of forgiveness isn't an intellectual process that can be learned by our egos.

The act of forgiveness is a very complex and personal experience. It's a "spiritual healing" that occurs deep within the subconsciousness at the soul level. Many of us are aware that forgiveness isn't a voluntary action, but an involuntary action. This means that our conscious minds can't decide exactly how, when, or where forgiveness will take place. Many of us have tried to forgive with our rational minds by writing logical letters of forgiveness or by simply telling someone that they are forgiven. Normally a few days afterwards, however, it's discovered that the feelings of anger and blame for the particular person who was being forgiven haven't disappeared. The reason the forgiveness didn't occur was because it was being performed at the shallow level of the ego and not at the deeper, spiritual level of the soul. True forgiveness will always be a spiritual experience, involving deep feelings of love, acceptance, and compassion. When true forgiveness occurs, both the offender and the offended will feel totally at peace about the harmful event.

The spiritual healing that occurs during forgiveness is very similar to a physical healing of the body. Both are miraculous, natural functions that occur over time, but only when the conditions are right. If the conditions aren't suitable, then a healing doesn't occur. The reason we see medical doctors when we are sick is to learn about the conditions that must be established so that a natural, physical healing can occur. Doctors don't heal us, but they do help us establish healing environments. Likewise, if we want an act of forgiveness to occur, we must establish an appropriate forgiving environment.

Developing a forgiving environment

In order for the forgiveness process to occur naturally, the following mental and physical conditions must be established.

1. *An identification of the person who requires forgiveness.*
   It's important to clearly identify the exact person you want to forgive. Concentrate on one person at a time. It's diffi-cult to forgive groups of people, even though you may believe that the group, as a whole, did you wrong.

2. *A clear perception of the harmful event.* It's helpful to visualize as many details of the harmful event as possible. This may be painful, but it's important to be in touch with the total situation. Accurate details are not required, because it's your perception of the person and his actions that are being addressed.

3. *An awareness of your feelings and thoughts about the event.* Recall the feelings and thoughts you had during the harmful event. Become aware of how you feel and think now about the situation. Get in touch with the deep-seated emotions you have experienced because of the event.

4. *A knowledge of why you want to forgive.* Without a good reason to forgive, many of us won't take the time to forgive another. Therefore, it's important to know how you will personally benefit from the act of forgiveness. Some people visualize what their lives will be like after the forgiveness has taken place, and use this image as the incentive for their actions.

5. *A desire and willingness to forgive.* For forgiveness to occur there must be a desire and a willingness to forgive. This doesn't always come easily. Some people don't want to forgive, because they enjoy the position of being a martyr. These people won't forgive until the benefits of being injured—the extra personal attention and consoling remarks—are overshadowed by the pain and inconvenience caused by the act of unforgiveness. Some people aren't willing to forgive, because they lack confidence in their own abilities to manage their daily lives. These people would rather blame the injurious activities of others for their daily problems. Whatever the situation may be, forgiveness doesn't occur until there is a desire and a willingness to forgive.

6. *A conducive physical environment.* Sometimes forgiveness can only occur when the physical environment has changed. For example, a young man living in his parents' house would have a difficult time forgiving his father for childhood abuse, if the father is still abusive towards him. Until the young man moves out of the house, it's unlikely that forgiveness will occur.

7. *An understanding that the person did the best he could.* Many of us have difficulty believing that a person who has committed an aggressive act against another was doing the best he could at the particular moment, but it's true. The actions of an aggressor are the result of his rational thinking. We are not in a position to judge the correctness of his actions, because we don't know all the facts and thoughts that went into his decision process. For example, the school bully who beats up a younger child may do so, because in his thinking, the action proves that he is stronger and more worthy than the younger child. In the bully's mind, what he is doing is correct, because the action increases his self-esteem.

8. *A realization that forgiveness takes time.* All deep wounds, whether physical or mental, take time to heal. Forgiveness, which is a spiritual healing, will occur in time, because your soul, the God within, wants it to occur. During the time of healing, it's important to avoid additional injuries to the wound. This can be accomplished through a simple prayer. Just pray and believe that a complete healing will take place, and it will.

One final comment about the act of forgiveness. If it's true that we're living our lives within divine plans, and that the people who are causing us difficulty are just our angelic friends in disguise, then how can we do anything else but forgive them for their human actions. Their human actions are helping our souls to grow. It's because of this belief that many people, including myself, now find it easy to forgive others.

Real forgiveness requires a resolution of all feelings to the point of equal honor for both parties. They must part with equal dignity. True forgiveness leaves the offender with as much innocence as the offended.

Richard Hanson

FOLLOW-UP EXERCISES

(1) Based on yesterday's inventory lesson, you should have a list of people you need to forgive. Try to develop a forgiving environment so that you can forgive these people. Are there some you don't want to forgive? Do you understand that these people really did the best they could under the circumstances?

(2) Write a short letter to those people you are ready to forgive and make your amends. If a person is deceased, still write a letter and say what you want to say. Their spirit will get your message. You will be pleasantly surprised at the freedom these letters will bring you.

—Day #11—

Increasing self-esteem through thoughts

A few years ago, I was at the Detroit airport waiting for a plane to San Francisco. As I sat in the lobby waiting, a well-dressed man came up to me and with a very confident voice said, "Are you Dave Lindsey?" I looked up from the magazine I was reading and saw a complete stranger. I told him I was Dave Lindsey and asked who he was. He introduced himself as Carl Jackson. The name rang a bell, but I couldn't place the face with the name. The only Carl Jackson I could recall was an extremely timid, overweight young man who attended the same college I attended many years ago. That Carl Jackson was too shy to approach another person sitting in an airport lobby. In fact, that Carl Jackson was so unsure of himself that he hardly ever talked to anyone.

So I said to the man in an inquisitive manner, "It's nice meeting you, Carl. What can I do for you?" He said that since we were both waiting for the same plane, that maybe we could pass the time by talking about the good old days. I finally said to him, "Carl, I'm sorry, I don't know who you are." He started to laugh and said, "Dave, don't you remember the withdrawn, sloppy-dressing man you went to college with? The young man who always sat in the back of the room and got embarrassed just from answering a question? It's me, Carl Jackson. Don't you remember?" I couldn't believe my eyes. It really was Carl Jackson. But it was a very different Carl. It was a Carl Jackson with poise and confidence.

After talking with him for several minutes, I asked him if he would mind if I had my seat assignment changed, so we could sit together on the plane. I told him I was very interested in learning how he had changed his personality so much since college, and would enjoy talking to him on the flight. He told me he was very proud of what he had accomplished and would like to share it with me. So I had my seat assignment changed, and we talked for the next four hours. During the flight he told me a fascinating story about how he was transformed from a shy person with low self-esteem to a confident corporate executive with high self-esteem. He told me his personal transformation started when he understood and accepted his childhood environment.

Carl started his story by describing the environment in which he grew up. He told me that when he was young, his parents and brother were totally absorbed in the game of golf. His father was a golf pro at the local country club; his mother was president of a women's golf association; and his brother was the "star" of the high school golf team. Carl said he hated golf as a child and had great difficulty even hitting a golf ball. He said he never felt important or worthy, because he couldn't do what the rest of the family considered important. Carl told me his parents often made fun of his inability to score well at golf, and jokingly suggested that maybe they took the wrong baby home from the hospital after Carl was born. The jokes had a major influence on Carl's self-esteem.

Carl told me he cried many nights as a child, because he didn't feel loved by his parents. He said his parents often told him they loved him, but he didn't _feel_ the nurturing love he needed. According to Carl, there were many times the family members were together, but for him, they weren't quality times. During family outings, his father would try to teach him how to hit golf balls, and his mother would talk about social events at the country club. Carl said, "No one would ever listen to me when I talked about the things I thought were important."

Carl told me he and his brother grew apart as his brother became popular at school because of his golf team activities. Being a "star" on the golf team greatly enhanced his brother's self-esteem. Carl felt as if his brother had become the shining example of the perfect son in his parents' eyes. He said he believed for many years that the only way he could ever become close to his family and receive the love he desperately needed was by learning how to be a better golfer. "It may sound silly today," Carl said, "but my self-esteem as a teenager was tied directly to my golf score. As my score got worse, my self-esteem went down. I never became a good golfer when I lived at home with my parents and, therefore, I never became confident about anything else I did."

I was very interested to learn how Carl had changed from a person with such low self-esteem to an apparently outgoing corporate executive. So I jokingly asked him if his golf game had improved. He laughed and told me that his self-esteem was no longer tied to his golf game. "If it were," he said, "I would still be one of the most unhappy people in the world. The truth is, I never play golf anymore. I never enjoyed the game before, and I don't enjoy it now. I no longer believe that golf is important in life. My self-esteem is now based on my own value system."

Carl told me that most of his personality change occurred shortly after leaving college. He said he read several good books on the subject, and learned that his low self-esteem was the direct result of his feelings of being unloved and unworthy as a child. He told me one day he was thinking about his past and realized that he actually was loved as a child. He came to realize that his parents just couldn't express their love to him in the manner he wanted it expressed. He said he finally realized that because of his parents' upbringing, they were unable to express love in a warm, affectionate way. "My parents weren't the hugging type," Carl said, "and I needed hugs as a child. My parents still aren't very affectionate, but I understand and accept it now. I know my parents love me. They just don't show it in the way I would like them to."

Carl told me that during most of his childhood he didn't feel worthy. He said as a child he believed his parents' distorted values about golf were correct. Carl said, "I had no reason to believe that my parents' value system was anything else but correct. As a child, I wasn't in a position to doubt or question what they thought was right. As a child, I was expected to just accept their beliefs and values. There were many times I was frustrated and disappointed with myself, because I fell short of their expectations." According to Carl, being an Eagle Scout and having straight A's in high school did nothing for his self-esteem, since his parents and brother didn't place much value on scholastic achievements. Golf was the only thing they valued. "My increase in self-esteem," Carl said, "came when I realized that my own value system was more important than my parents' value system. My value system says that spiritual involvement, a happy home life, and honest business achievements are much more important in life than golf. Since I'm doing very well in these areas of life, my self-esteem is very high. It's unfortunate, but true, that many people are unhappy today, because they are trying to live up to the meaningless values of their friends and relatives."

It was quite obvious to me that Carl was very proud of who he was and how well he had overcome an unhealthy childhood environment. I personally found it interesting that he had done it without years of professional help. So I said to Carl, "I would like to use your story someday when I talk to people about self-esteem. I would like to tell people how self-esteem can be greatly enhanced without professional help, if a person is motivated and committed to change." Carl turned to me and said softly, "It won't be true if you tell people that. I had professional help. In fact, I had the very best professional help. I had God helping me. My self-esteem grew when I learned how to meditate. It was through my spiritual meditations, my conversations with the God within, that I learned that I'm totally loved at all times. Through meditation, I have learned that I'm a very important and worthy spiritual being, and a significant part of God's grand plan. It has been through conversations with my soul, that I have learned that low self-esteem is just an erroneous human thought that is based on incorrect judgments and values. I have learned that low self-esteem can be completely eliminated by the unconditional loving of others. It's through the unconditional loving and serving of others, that my self-esteem has blossomed." My eyes started to tear as I listened to Carl's sincere words of wisdom. Carl had sure come a long way since our college days.

As we approached the San Francisco airport, I asked Carl how his brother was doing. I was interested in learning if his brother's self-esteem was maintained at a high level after being a golf star in high school. I wasn't surprised to hear from Carl that his brother wasn't doing well. Apparently, his brother had done the same thing

Carl had done. He had tied his self-esteem directly to his golfing abilities. Carl told me that when his brother's golf career ended because of a medical problem, his brother became very depressed and lost confidence in his ability to handle even the simplest problems.

I have often thought about that plane trip and the four hours that Carl and I spent together. Was it just a coincidence or was there some divine reason for us to share our personal stories with each other? We both got in touch with some deep feelings on that trip. Carl taught me several practical and spiritual lessons during our short time together. A statement that Carl made at the end of the trip that I'll probably never forget is, "In God's eyes, we're all equally loved and worthy and, therefore, we should never consider ourselves to be greater or less than anyone else."

In God's eyes, we're all equally loved and worthy and, therefore, we should never consider ourselves to be greater or less than anyone else.

Developing self-esteem

By definition, self-esteem is how one feels about oneself. It's the overall judgment or belief that we have about ourselves and our abilities. We all have self-esteem. Unfortunately, some of us just don't seem to have enough to be able to live happy fulfilling lives. Have you ever thought about how much your self-esteem affects your life? It actually affects just about everything you do. Your self-esteem determines such things as who your friends are, how you live, what kind of job you have, what type of clothes you wear, and what you do on vacation. It also affects how people treat you, and how you treat them. It affects just about every decision you make. It also greatly influences whether or not you're successful in life.

The importance of self-esteem can't be overstated. The feelings and actions associated with self-esteem have a major impact on your happiness. With few exceptions, people with low self-esteem are less happy than people with high self-esteem. This is because their low self-esteem interferes with their successful interactions with other people. Usually, as a person's self-esteem increases, so does the person's overall happiness. Self-esteem is one of the keys to happiness.

Since self-esteem is an attitude or feeling about oneself, it's subject to change. You weren't born with a certain amount of self-esteem and expected to live a lifetime with that given quantity. Self-esteem is a fluctuating self-attitude that changes with every daily occurrence. You have the power to increase or decrease your self-esteem anytime you want. You can increase your self-esteem just by changing your beliefs about yourself and your environment. You don't need to go to a special place and accomplish an important task to increase your self-esteem. All you have to do is go within, to the roots of your self-esteem, and make some minor changes in your belief system. Self-esteem and happiness are "inside jobs."

It's very important to understand that self-esteem is based on how one feels about oneself at a particular moment. It's a "now" feeling about oneself. Your current level of self-esteem isn't the result of how much love and worthiness you felt as a child, but is a direct consequence of your ability to change and grow. Although it's true that your childhood experiences did have a significant effect on how high your self-esteem was when you entered adulthood, those early experiences don't dictate the level of self-esteem you can reach. The magnitude of self-esteem that you'll obtain in life is determined by your commitment and desire to change. If you're committed to change, change will definitely occur. It's possible for each of us to overcome our childhood experiences and develop high self-esteem.

I told you the story about my old college friend Carl, because he is a living example of what a person can do to increase self-esteem. Carl made a commitment to change his attitude about himself. He told me during our plane trip together that he didn't enjoy life when he was in college, because of his low self-esteem.

He was unhappy because he had great difficulty interacting with the other students. It was because of his unhappiness that he read self-help books about self-esteem and learned how to change his attitude towards himself. The first thing that Carl did was to learn why he had low self-esteem. The reasons most people have low self-esteem are because they don't feel loved and they don't feel worthy. People who don't feel worthy, believe that their actions in life are unimportant and lack value. They also feel they are incapable of successfully accomplishing new projects. To have high self-esteem, we must feel both loved and worthy.

You can demonstrate to yourself that you are actually loved and worthy by completing the *Self-Esteem Fact Sheet* at the end of this lesson. This fact sheet has helped many people to discover that they are capable of giving and receiving love, and that they are capable of accomplishing important tasks in their lives. The first three questions on the fact sheet address the "lovability" of a person. The questions are: *(1) Who do I love?*, *(2) Who loves me?*, and *(3) Whose love do I doubt?* After honestly completing this section of the fact sheet, most people are in touch with the fact that they are very lovable. Most people learn that there is a great deal of love flowing between them and others. Maybe the love isn't always expressed in the manner they would like it expressed, but the love is there. If our egos weren't in the way of our loving feelings, we would find that love naturally flows between us and every other thing on Earth. Each of us is a loving Spiritual Being. Each of us is "pure love" trying to express itself.

Many people have difficulty completing Part B of the *Self-Esteem Fact Sheet*. This section, which deals with worthiness, causes problems, because most people look for major accomplishments. But it's the insignificant things that one does in life with a loving attitude that are the important accomplishments. Reading a bedtime story to a child, visiting a sick friend at the hospital, and being involved in a charitable event are typical of the accomplishments that bring real worth to a person. These are the types of events that should be listed on the fact sheet in response to the statement, *Things I have accomplished.* After completing the second part of the fact sheet, most people have discovered that they are very worthy and capable. Most people have also discovered that they have brought a great deal of happiness to others.

After the fact sheet has been completed, it should be kept in a place where it can be reviewed and up-dated daily. The more you look at your fact sheet, the more you'll realize that you're a very lovable and worthy person. The more you believe in yourself, the higher your self-esteem will become. The spiritual Law of Thought, which we discussed on Day #3, states:

What you think--is what you are.

You can take advantage of this spiritual law and allow it to work for you. You can fill your mind with positive thoughts about how lovable and worthy you are, and then allow loving and worthy experiences to come into your life. These experiences will automatically occur, if you believe they will. When you totally believe in something, it happens. If you think you are lovable and worthy, you're going to quickly discover that you are lovable and worthy. The level of your self-esteem depends solely on your thoughts. Since your self-esteem is controlled by the thoughts of your mind, just by changing your thoughts, you can change your self-esteem.

Since your self-esteem is controlled by the thoughts of your mind, just by changing your thoughts, you can change your self-esteem.

Increasing self-esteem through meditation

Some of you may feel trapped in the vicious circle of low self-esteem. You intellectually analyze your thoughts about yourself, and come to the erroneous conclusion that you're unlovable and unworthy. Based on this conclusion, your thoughts are very negative about yourself and your ability to successfully interact with others. Because your life experiences are a direct reflection of your thoughts, you may have found that it's very difficult to emerge from this state of negativity. The only way I know of stepping above this condition is by having positive, loving experiences with others. For some of you who have very low self-esteem, you may think it's impossible to have such an experience with another person. If you feel this way, I would suggest that you first have a positive, loving experience with yourself. I suggest that you try meditation. Meditation, which will be discussed in the next lesson, is a wonderful way to learn how important and loved you really are. Many shy people have greatly increased their self-esteem by having positive, loving experiences with themselves during meditations.

Many shy people have greatly increased their self-esteem by having positive, loving experiences with themselves during meditations.

FOLLOW-UP EXERCISES

(1) Complete Part A of the *Self-Esteem Fact Sheet* as thoroughly as possible. Get in touch with the feelings of love that flow between you and others. If you have love for a particular pet or plant, list them under the *Who do I love?* heading. Are you more lovable than you thought you were?

(2) Complete Part B of the *Self-Esteem Fact Sheet*. List all your accomplishments that involved the feelings of love. These are the accomplishments that bring true worth to an individual. Only include the actions that you value under the heading of *Things I will accomplish*. Too often we try to achieve things just to satisfy someone else's value system. Review your fact sheet daily.

SELF-ESTEEM FACT SHEET

Directions: Please answer the following questions as honestly as possible.

PART A: LOVABILITY FACTS

WHO DO I LOVE?

1
2
3
4
5
6
7
8
9
10

WHO LOVES ME?

1
2
3
4
5
6
7
8
9
10

WHOSE LOVE DO I DOUBT?

1
2
3
4
5
6
7
8
9
10

PART B: WORTHINESS FACTS

THINGS I HAVE ACCOMPLISHED

1
2
3
4
5
6
7
8
9
10
11
12
13
14
15

THINGS I WILL ACCOMPLISH

1
2
3
4
5
6
7
8
9
10
11
12
13
14
15

—Day #12—

Finding inner peace through meditation

How would you feel if God appeared in your room right now and answered all your questions about life? How would you feel if you were personally told by the Holy Spirit that you didn't have to worry about anything, because you'll always have everything you'll need in life to be happy? How would you feel if you knew that when death occurred, you would peacefully return home to the heavens? If you can get in touch with these extraordinary feelings, then you'll understand why more and more people are meditating. The people who deeply meditate, normally have these incredible feelings. The feelings are generally those of being totally loved and protected. Would you like to experience these feelings on a daily basis? You can, if you learn how to meditate.

The type of meditation we're going to discuss in this lesson is purely a Christian meditation. It has nothing to do with any other religion or teachings. However, it does require a certain belief, a strong desire to obtain insight about one's life, and a commitment of time. In order to have a deeply fulfilling Christian meditation, a person must believe that there is a spiritual power greater than his "human-self" that can be contacted. This spiritual power actually does exist and is known by many names. It's often referred to as the Holy Spirit, the Holy Ghost, the Higher Power, the Christ Consciousness, and the God Within.

There are many passages in the Bible where Jesus talked about this spiritual power and the purpose of its existence. One of the passages is John 14:26, where Jesus said:

The Counselor, the Holy Spirit, whom the Father will send in my name, will teach you all things and will remind you of everything I have said to you.

The Holy Spirit that Jesus talked about is within you. It's not some mystical entity that comes from deep space and visits you occasionally during times of trouble. It's the Spiritual Being portion of your "total being" that was discussed in an earlier lesson. The Holy Spirit is that part of God that lives within each of us. The fact that God lives within you is not a New Age idea. In the New Testament, in 1 Corinthians 6:19, we're told exactly where the Holy Spirit resides. The verse says:

Do you not know that your body is a temple of the Holy Spirit, <u>who is in you,</u> whom you have received from God?

The Bible is saying that living within each of us is a spiritual counselor who will teach us everything we need to know about living a life in accordance with Jesus' teachings. Since Jesus' teachings were mainly about God, love, and peace, we can learn more about these subjects by communicating with our personal counselor, the Holy Spirit. In my opinion, the best way to communicate with this spiritual power is by having deep, loving meditations from the heart. It's important that the feelings of the heart are expressed in meditation, and not the intellectual thoughts of the mind. In the Bible, in Psalms 19:14, it talks about meditating from the heart when it says:

Let the words of my mouth, and the meditations of my heart, be acceptable in thy sight, O Lord.

Would you like to learn more about the teachings of Jesus? Would you like to learn about His teachings of love and peace directly from the God within, instead of hearing them second-hand from a minister or priest? Would you like to have a one-on-one conversation with the Holy Spirit, and have this Spirit answer personal questions you have about yourself and your life on Earth? Then learn how to meditate. Christian meditation is a spiritual two-way communication between you and the Holy Spirit that resides within you.

Christian meditation is a spiritual two-way communication between you and the Holy Spirit that resides within you.

Levels of meditation

I have never been able to find two people who totally agree on what meditation is and how it should be performed. Even the meditation books being sold today present totally different thoughts about meditation. The information found in books dealing with Christian meditation is quite different than the information in books on Transcendental Meditation and Hindu meditation. So let's start with the dictionary definition of meditation and build from there. According to the dictionary, acceptable definitions for meditation are:

(1) The dwelling on anything in thought.
(2) The act of deep, continued thought.
(3) Serious contemplation; mental reflection.
(4) Deep reflection on sacred matters as a devotional act.

The above definitions are really quite different. They describe various levels or intensities of the meditation process. Yet, these are the types of definitions that most people have in their minds when they talk about meditation. I have a friend who says he meditates every morning as he drives to work. According to him, what he does is "think" about his daily work activities, and tries to determine in his mind the most efficient way of performing his duties. Based on definition #1, he is meditating, but yet, he is doing it at such a conscious level that he is still able to drive a car. I have another friend who is at the other extreme. Some people think he is a religious fanatic. He deeply meditates for about two hours everyday. He has a special room in his house where he sits partially naked on a straw mat and chants. His chants are secret words that were given to him by some organization. His meditations are so deep, however, that he is unaware of the activities that are going on around him. When he says he meditates, he is talking about a meditation that is best defined by definition #4.

While it's true that both of these friends meditate daily, the benefits they receive from their meditations are quite different. My friend who meditates superficially on an intellectual level, receives superficial, intellectual information during his meditations. On the other hand, my friend who meditates at a deeper, feeling level, receives guidance from his Higher Power at a spiritual level. Through meditation, this friend has become aware of the importance of loving everything about life and everyone in it. He is a total joy to be around. His attitude is very positive, and he never seems to worry about anything. He is always loving and helpful.

This deeper level of meditation that brings spiritual guidance is the type of meditation we'll be addressing during the rest of this lesson. I'm not going to suggest that anyone meditates for two hours in their shorts, but I'm going to encourage you to try to meditate at a "feeling level" instead of a superficial "thinking level." Deep meditation is more of a feeling process than a thought process. Several thoughts may be involved at the beginning of a meditation experience, but as the meditation progresses, one's intuitive feeling nature takes over and determines the direction and intensity of the meditation. Meditation is a natural "feeling" experience that will help you develop intimate relationships with God, yourself, and nature.

Meditation is a natural "feeling" experience that will help you develop intimate relationships with God, yourself, and nature.

Benefits of a Christian meditation

There are so many personal benefits that are gained from a deep Christian meditation that if I listed them all, some people would start wondering what the catch is. The truth is, there is no catch. There are no costs or special clothes to wear. There are no secret chants or rituals to perform. Meditation is just a natural activity that God has given us the ability to perform. As stated earlier, all we need is a belief that there is a higher power that can be contacted (the Holy Spirit, the God within, etc.), a strong desire to obtain insight about our lives, and a commitment of time. That is all.

If you are able to satisfy the above three requirements and are willing to meditate, you're going to personally discover many of the benefits that other spiritual meditators have discovered. The benefits will be in every area of your life, not just in the spiritual arena. There will be enormous psychological, physiological, and sociological benefits. The greatest benefit of deep Christian meditation is the indescribable feeling of joy that comes from knowing that you can talk directly to God whenever you desire. If you have a personal problem, concern, or fear and want some guidance, just go into meditation and ask why the problem has occurred and how it can be resolved. You'll probably be given an immediate answer. Meditation is a much better way than prayer for obtaining information and resolving problems. This is because meditation is a two-way conversation with the God within, whereas, prayer is a one-way request with usually no immediate known response. At the end of a prayer, often the person who is praying, doesn't know what the response will be. In meditation, however, the response normally comes during the same meditative session in which the question was asked. Spiritual guidance appears to be more readily given through meditation than prayer.

There are many personal benefits obtained from meditation. Some of them are the following:

PSYCHOLOGICAL:

increases in: positive attitude, emotional stability, self-esteem, self-confidence, lovableness, tolerance, innovation, creativity, naturalness, intuitiveness

decreases in: anxiety, depression, feelings of unlovableness

PHYSIOLOGICAL:

increases in: ability to sleep, ability to relax

SOCIOLOGICAL:

increases in: sociability, respect for others, cordiality, tolerance

decreases in: social inadequacy, irritability, rigidity, anxiety

You shouldn't expect all the above improvements to happen the first time you have a deep Christian meditation, but they will probably all occur after a few months of daily involvement. Meditation will also help you to appreciate nature more. Through meditation, you'll learn that we're all one, and there is no separation between us and our natural environment. You'll learn that everything on Earth is spiritually connected. The Spirit of God isn't just in humans, but is in everything. Meditation is a wonderful way to learn about love and life. It's a spiritual experience that will improve every area of your life.

Meditation is a spiritual experience that will improve every area of your life.

How to meditate

It's difficult to tell someone how to perform a natural function. If you asked me how to run, I could explain it in one minute or in sixty minutes. The sixty minute explanation would include such things as the type of shoes to wear, how to breathe correctly, and where to do it. It's very possible that the sixty minute explanation might be so complex and confusing that it would interfere with the enjoyment of the running experience. A similar problem exists in explaining to someone how to meditate. A short explanation may not be adaquate, however, a long explanation may be so confusing that it reduces the pleasure and intensity of the meditative experience. Therefore, I'll just give you a short general explanation on how to meditate, and then tell you in limited detail how I do it. Below are the seven steps for a Christian meditation.

STEPS FOR A CHRISTIAN MEDITATION

(1) Allow yourself 30 minutes of uninterrupted time in a quiet, dimly-lit room. The best time is usually in the morning before the mind becomes too involved in the daily activities.

(2) Turn on some soft music. There are many special meditation tapes on the market today that are very helpful.

(3) Find a comfortable body position which allows you to totally relax, but still remain alert. This can be a sitting position or a lying down position. Most instructors on meditation will strongly recommend that the meditator sits in a straight chair or on the ground.

(4) Close your eyes. Take several long, deep breaths, and while doing this, concentrate on some aspect of God. This could be a beautiful visual scene in nature, a feeling of love for someone or something, or it could be the mesmerizing sounds from the meditation tape. Concentrate on this aspect of God until you feel that your body is totally relaxed. This may take 10 or 15 minutes.

(5) When you are totally relaxed and while your eyes are closed, visually look at a point in the middle of your forehead. Keep your eyes closed at all times. While doing this, ask God to make Himself present to you. This is done by consciously saying or thinking a special prayer or spiritual words. Say the words over and over again until God appears. The words should be whatever you are "feeling" in your heart at that particular time. The meditation moves from a "thinking" to a "feeling" experience as you say the words. Typical words are, "Dear Heavenly Father," "Lord Jesus," and "May God bless me with His presence." In time, God will appear in your meditations in the form of a bright white light. How soon God appears in your meditations is dependent upon your beliefs about the spiritual world. In the New Testament, there are several passages that state that God is Light.

(6) Once you are "in the Light," ask the questions that are in your heart, and wait for the answers. The answers will come as thoughts or as softly spoken words. Be prepared to accept and obey the answers. The Holy Spirit, the God within, knows what is best for you and your soul.

(7) End the meditation by telling God what you're feeling in your heart. God already knows what is in your heart, but by saying it, you'll become more in touch with what you're feeling.

The author's meditation technique

Before I explain to you how I meditate, I would like to tell you about a discussion I had a few days ago at a men's support group meeting. At the meeting, I was asked two thought provoking questions. The questions were, "What has been your greatest personal disappointment?" and "What has been your greatest accomplishment?" It didn't take me very long to come up with the correct answers, because I had thought about those same two questions several times before. My greatest disappointment occurred during the first forty years of my life, and was my willingness to be a conformist. It was my willingness to do exactly what everyone else was doing. During those years, I disregarded my individuality and followed the crowd. I let myself be controlled by the opinions and beliefs of others. Often, I didn't even know who the "others" were who had established the rules and practices I was following. For many years, I was a clone of society. I mention this now, because some people have told me they don't meditate, because the practice isn't supported by their church. I believe that each of us has the right and the responsibility to decide for ourself which spiritual practices are appropriate. There is no one living on Earth who is more holy or spiritually closer to God than you are.

My answer to the question on "greatest accomplishment" was learning how to communicate with the God within. It was learning how to meditate. Meditation is now the most important thing I do each day. So let me share with you how I prepare for meditation and what my meditations are like. From these descriptions, you may get a better feeling about what to expect from your meditations.

I begin preparing for my morning meditation about 30 minutes before I actually start the process. To clear my mind of forthcoming daily events, I will often read a chapter from an inspirational book, or sometimes I'll just think peaceful thoughts. Normally, I avoid reading the morning newspaper before meditation, because the stories in the newspaper are often unpleasant. When I feel very peaceful, I'll go to my den and complete the final preparations. This includes positioning several pillows on the floor and turning on a meditation tape.

The audio tape I play is called *Golden Voyage* (Volume 3) by Awakening Productions. The tape contains tranquil sounds of nature, as well as beautiful background music. The room I use for meditation is dimly lit and contains a large picture of Christ and some inspirational wall plaques. When I'm ready to start the meditation, I lie down on the pillows, facing the ceiling with my arms outstretched and with my legs crossed at the ankles. Within a short time, my physical body becomes very relaxed. My mind, however, stays alert in anticipation of a spiritual experience.

I then close my eyes and take several long, deep breaths. Often at this stage, random intellectual thoughts will invade my mind. I have learned through experience to just let the thoughts drift in my mind without addressing them. The thoughts always go away within a few minutes. As my physical body becomes more relaxed, my breathing becomes slower and slower. When my breathing is very slow, I focus my total attention, with my eyes closed, on a point in the middle of my lower forehead. This point is known to some meditators as the Christ Consciousness Center, because it's believed to be the position of the single eye of light that Christ talked about in the Bible. This position is also known to some meditators as the location of the sixth chakra or the third eye. It's during the concentration on this position that I feel a separation between my mind and my physical body. It's at this stage that I ask God to make Himself present.

I ask God to make me aware of His presence by saying in my mind the following words over and over again until the Light of God appears. I say, "Dear Heavenly Father, this is your servant Dave, please come forward and help me." Within a few minutes the light appears. I believe, based on the teachings from the Bible, that this light is the Holy Spirit. While I'm "in the Light," I ask God questions, and I usually get answers. Often in meditation, I'm given instructions to do things. Sometimes I'm told to write letters to people who need help. Sometimes I'm told to call someone on the phone and give them support. Sometimes I'm told to just enjoy the day with the family. Several times I have been told to write this book. Whatever I'm told to do in meditation, I always do. I have learned that the more I listen and obey the Light, the more the Light responds to my daily needs.

As my meditation comes to an end, I normally express my feelings of gratitude to God for my wonderful life. I usually tell Him exactly what I'm feeling at the particular moment. The feelings that I have near the end of a meditative session are always those of love and peace. Even after the meditation is over, those same feelings often stay with me for the rest of the day.

Although some people may consider my meditations to be fairly deep, it's my understanding that I'm just touching the outer surface of what is possible. Hopefully, as the years come and go, I'll become more knowledgeable about the art of meditation and will discover more of the universe that exists within me. In my opinion, meditation is a natural, effortless way to learn about God's spiritual universe, which exists within each of us.

Meditation is a natural, effortless way to learn about God's spiritual universe, which exists within each of us.

FOLLOW-UP EXERCISES

(1) Meditate 30 minutes a day for the next several days and see what happens. You may experience many of the benefits that are listed in this lesson. Develop your own procedure for meditating, or follow the seven steps for a Christian meditation. Relax and enjoy.

(2) Make a note to read the following books on Christian meditation.
—*Christian Meditation, Its Art and Practice* by H. W. Pipkin.
—*The Art of Meditation* by Joel S. Goldsmith.

—Day #13—

Discovering what makes you happy

Do you know what makes you happy? Think about it for a few minutes. What is it that really makes you happy? Is it money? Is it friends? Is it being successful? Surprisingly, most of us think we know what brings us happiness, yet many of us are unable to write a list of nonconflicting items that would make us happy. Too often our lists include conflicting statements such as being president of a company and having lots of free time for the family. Discovering what really makes us happy isn't an easy task.

Several years ago I attended a seminar called *How to be Successful.* The leader of the seminar was a very charismatic young executive who had become well known in the field of electronics. This man had earned five college degrees, had been awarded several patents, and had written a number of technical articles for magazines. The man was obviously very intelligent and very successful in his field. From the stories he told us, it was also apparent that he was very wealthy.

During the seminar, this energetic leader told us that if we wanted to be happy in life, all we had to do was to lead respectable personal lives and be dedicated to our work. According to this seminar leader, happiness would come to each of us if we were successful at our jobs. The seminar was filled with many facts and figures that indicated that financial success was important for happiness. We were told during the seminar that most domestic arguments were over money and, therefore, it's important to make as much money as possible to guarantee a happy family life. The seminar leader also told us that if we expected to be financially independent by the time we retired, we must be willing to commit at least sixty hours a week to our professions. We were told that the keys to success and happiness were commitment, desire, goal setting, and action.

By the time the morning session was over, I was somewhat confused. Was my overall happiness that dependent on my success at work? Were the "workaholic" ideas presented that morning the best philosophy for living? Would I be happy working 60 hours a week in order to be financially independent by retirement age? At this stage of the seminar, I was very uncomfortable with the concepts being presented.

During the afternoon session, we were asked to separate into small groups and to discuss what success and happiness meant to us. This was a very interesting exercise. It seemed as if none of the eight people in my group could agree on what success and happiness were. Some of us thought that success and happiness were related to each other, while others thought that the two were completely independent. A couple of us agreed that happiness was the result of being successful, while others thought that being successful was the result of being happy. It was at this point of disagreement, that the seminar leader announced to everyone that we had 15 minutes to develop meaningful definitions for "success" and "happiness," and that we would be sharing our definitions with the class. This announcement caused our group to panic. It was becoming embarrassing. None of us could believe that we were having so much trouble defining two concepts that were so important to us.

During the next 15 minutes, there was a lot of bickering within our group. Our egos had taken control of the exercise and were doing their best to save us from being embarrassed in front of the entire class. As soon as a definition was suggested, it would be viciously attacked. One of the college students said that happiness to him would be having a million dollars. At this comment, an older man took out his checkbook and wrote a check for a million dollars. He gave the check to the student and asked him to sit in the corner with the check and see if he was any happier just knowing he had money. Obviously, the point that the older man was trying to make to the student was that just having additional money would not make him any happier. We debated for 15 minutes and never came up with good definitions.

When it was time to read our definitions to the entire class, no one wanted to do it. Our definitions weren't very impressive to say the least. Fortunately, the young college student was man enough to stand up and tell the rest of the seminar attendees that none of us totally understood the relationship between success and happiness. He said we all had our own individual ideas about what the two words meant and couldn't agree on common definitions. To my surprise, most of the other groups had similar comments.

The seminar leader wasn't disappointed by the responses of the individual groups. In fact, he told us that most groups in previous seminars also had difficulty defining the relationship between success and happiness. He even told us that the philosophy he presented during the morning session, that suggested that success brings happiness, may not always be true. He indicated that in spite of all his material wealth and personal recognition, he wasn't quite as happy as he used to be. His honest disclosure was greatly appreciated by the class.

Does success bring happiness?

One of the main reasons there are so many unhappy people in our society today is because many of us have never taken the time to discover what makes us happy. Chances are if you ask a friend what makes him happy, you'll get a very superficial answer that involves material objects such as money, a new house, or a fancy car. Or you may get a more profound answer that includes such words as God and love. You may not even get an answer. Most people have a very difficult time stating exactly what makes them happy, because they have never really thought about it. Most of us plow through life day after day trying to be <u>successful</u> instead of trying to be <u>happy.</u> There is a major difference between being successful and being happy.

A successful person isn't necessarily a happy person. However, a happy person is always a successful person. Just because a happy person may not live in a mansion or drive a fancy car doesn't mean the person isn't successful. It only means the person understands that material wealth is not part of the equation for happiness. Society has done itself a great injustice by glorifying success more so than happiness.

In the dictionary, success and happiness are defined as follows:

SUCCESS (1) A favorable or satisfactory outcome or result.
     (2) The gaining of wealth, fame, rank, etc.
       The synonyms are: accomplishment, attainment, renown, achievement, winner, prosperity, wealth, and affluence.

HAPPINESS (1) Having feelings of great pleasure, joy, and contentment.
     (2) The enjoyment of pleasure without pain. The synonyms are: cheerfulness, light-heartedness, joyfulness, jubilation, bliss, exhilaration, and gaiety.

From the above definitions, it's quite obvious that success and happiness are two different concepts. Yet, many of us use the words interchangeably when we set goals. One minute we say we want to be successful, and the next minute we say we want to be happy. Being successful, doesn't necessarily mean being happy. I have a very wealthy friend who works in his machine shop seventy hours a week producing special production parts for the automotive industry. He is well known for his expertise in this area. He is also extremely unhappy. I have never seen him laugh or show loving feelings for anyone. He is also constantly worried about obtaining future business. When the automotive industry slows down, he has difficulty finding enough work to keep his employees busy. By society's standards, he is a very successful person but, unfortunately, he is also very unhappy.

I have a sister-in-law named Sonia, who earns less than fifty dollars a week teaching music classes to preschool children. She gave up a prestigious job with General Motors when she was expecting her first child. She totally enjoys her current roles as wife, mother, music teacher, and volunteer music director of her church's Sunday school classes. She has an active life filled with family activities, hobbies, friends, and work. She never worries about the future because, as she puts it, "I have faith that God will always take care of me." By society's standards, she would be considered a very happy person, but maybe not a successful person. By my standards, she is one of the most successful people I know, because she is doing exactly what she wants to do at this particular time in her life. Maybe her accomplishments will never appear on the front page of any newspaper, but her accomplishments will appear in the hearts of the children she teaches.

If we're to enjoy life to the fullest, we must decide what is more important to us. Is it more important to be happy in life, or is it more important to be successful? Is it more important to be contented and joyful, or is it more important to be wealthy and famous? It's possible to have it all. However, to be both happy and successful in life, we must first learn how to be happy, and then allow success to follow.

To be both happy and successful in life, we must first learn how to be happy, and then allow success to follow.

Determining what makes you happy

Up until a few years ago, when someone asked me what made me happy, I would answer by rattling off several items that brought me happiness. I would tell people the things that make me happy were my relationships with my wife and son, being with friends, going to parties, fishing, boating, my new car, and several other material objects. It seemed as if my answers were always acceptable to my friends who were asking the questions. If someone had asked me a few years ago what was the one most important thing that brought me happiness, I wouldn't have been able to answer the question. I had never thought about it before. Most of us never take the time to discover what it is that really brings us happiness. Think about it for a few minutes. What is the one most important thing that brings you happiness? What is it that brings you the greatest pleasure, joy, and contentment? This isn't a trick question with a single universal answer. What brings one person deep feelings of happiness isn't necessarily the same thing that brings another person great pleasure and joy. It's very important, however, for each of us to understand what it is that brings us happiness. It's from this understanding that we'll become happy and successful in life.

I have spent a lot of time during the past couple of years determining what really makes me happy. As a result of my efforts, I have become a very happy person. My mood swings are normally from happy to very happy. I have very few down moments. If something happens that causes me some discomfort, I will look within the event for a spiritual lesson, and then bounce right back to a state of happiness.

It may be helpful in your quest for happiness to understand the procedure I went through in determining what brings me the greatest happiness. Some of you may end up with the same answers I did. Most of you will undoubtedly discover different answers. It doesn't matter that your findings are different. What is important is that you reestablish your priorities in life in order to emphasize the things that bring you the greatest happiness.

I realized what brought me the greatest happiness when I answered the following question: *"If I won the state lottery and was guaranteed two million dollars a year for the rest of my life, what would I do with my life?"* I wrote a list of about thirty things I would do once I had complete financial freedom. Only two of the items on the list were about buying something for myself. Most of the items I listed were about helping others. To be even more specific, they were about helping others to discover their spirituality. After determining that teaching spiritual principles was the main thing that brought me happiness, I reprioritized all my personal goals. The reason I'm so happy today is because I'm living a life with a central theme of helping others grow spiritually. I'm doing exactly what brings me the most happiness.

Most of you are going to discover that the things that bring you the greatest happiness are the activities that allow you to give and receive love. Love is the foundation of happiness. No matter how many material possessions you have, if you don't have a loving relative or friend to share them with, you're not going to totally enjoy your possessions. Happiness comes from the sharing of possessions, not from having possessions. Happiness is an inner feeling that blossoms from other inner feelings, such as love, joy, and peace.

What would you do if you won the state lottery and was guaranteed two million dollars a year for the rest of your life? I'm sure that many of you would spend some of the money on material possessions such as a new car or possibly a new house. Some of you would take a long vacation or travel around the world. This is fine. But with complete financial freedom, what would you do with the rest of your life? Would you quit your job? Would you get involved in another type of business? Would you work for a particular charity? Would you be more devoted to the needs of the elderly or disabled children? What would you do? It's important to understand exactly what you would do and why you would do it. Your personal happiness depends on this understanding.

Your happiness depends on your willingness to go into action, and do the things that make you happy.

FOLLOW-UP EXERCISES

(1) Congratulations! You have just won the state lottery and will receive two million dollars a year for the rest of your life. To collect the money, all you have to do is write a list of thirty things you are going to do now that you have financial freedom. Put a lot of thought into your list.

(2) Carefully examine the list you completed in the above exercise. Can you determine from the list what really brings you happiness? Is there a strong desire to help others or get involved with certain organizations or charities? Are you interested in traveling or continuing your education? The things that really bring you happiness are probably on this list. The events that bring most people happiness don't require two million dollars a year, but are often free.

—Day #14—

Doing what makes you happy

Last year while attending a local church, a stranger named John came up to me and asked if I would help him resolve some personal problems. He said he had heard some of my lectures a few years earlier about living a more fulfilling life, and thought that maybe I had some unique information that would help him become a happier person. I told John I really didn't have any special information, but would be willing to help him anyway I could. I invited John to join me for lunch the next day so we could talk. He accepted the invitation, and we agreed to meet at 12:30 at a local Mexican restaurant.

At 12:25, I arrived at the restaurant. I looked around to see if John was there, but he wasn't, so I sat down and waited. At 1:15, John drifted in. He didn't say anything about being 45 minutes late, so I just accepted it and thought that maybe it couldn't have been avoided. We sat down and had a delicious meal together. As we talked in the restaurant, I learned a great deal about John. In fact, it would probably be more accurate to say that I was amazed by John's general knowledge and talents. Although he wasn't formally educated, he had a great wealth of information about current events, history, and science. According to John, his personal talents were in the fields of poetry and music. He told me he had written over one hundred poems and was able to play seven different musical instuments.

As I listened to John talk about his poetry and music, I became aware of the joy and exhilaration he was experiencing. It was quite obvious to me that these two areas of his life were very important to him and brought him great pleasure. After about 15 minutes of listening to him talk, I finally said, "John, why did you want to see me today? Is there a problem you wanted to discuss?" John sat back in his chair and with a sorrowful voice said, "I want to talk to you about how unhappy I am." It was like I was suddenly hearing a different person. John's mood had swung from exuberance to self-pity within a few seconds. I was getting mixed signals, and I wasn't sure what to think.

So I asked John to describe his personal life to me. He told me he was married and had two wonderful children. He said that although he loved his wife and children, his family life wasn't as enjoyable as it used to be. He said he held himself responsible for the deterioration of the family life, because he was just too "wiped out" at the end of the work day to be a caring father and a loving husband. I asked John to describe his job to me. He told me he was the manager of his father's print shop. He said the only reason he took the job when he graduated from high school was because he thought his parents wanted him to. John told me he never enjoyed the work, and really didn't manage the business very well. According to John, he was too unorganized to run a printing business. He said because he was normally late with most of the orders, he didn't get a lot of repeat business. His comment about being late didn't surprise me, considering how late he was for our lunch.

I asked John if he became more organized would he be happier as a manager in the printing business. He thought for awhile and then said, "No." He told me that since his heart really wasn't in the business, he didn't think he would ever be happy working in the print shop. With tears in his eyes, John looked at me and said, "Dave, what I really want to do is write poetry during the day, and play a guitar in a band at night. I'm good in these two areas. I know I am. God gave me special talents in these areas. I know if I had the opportunity to do those things, I would be much happier, and my family life would probably be more fulfilling."

So, I asked John what was stopping him from making a career

change. He was obviously prepared for this question, and quickly rattled off about ten reasons why he couldn't do it. Some of his reasons were his parents would be disappointed if he left the family business, his wife would be concerned about their financial security, he didn't have a music agent to help him find a job in a band, and he didn't know how to get his poetry published.

I asked John to stop talking for a minute and to think about the excuses he was giving me for not making a career change. Then I said to him, "John, you know you have some unique God-given talents that you could be using to bring yourself happiness. Isn't it possible that the only reasons you're not making the career change are because you don't believe in yourself and you don't believe in your spiritual powers? All the reasons you have given me are scapegoats. Not one of them is a good reason why you shouldn't make the career change. Think about it." John thought about it for several minutes, and then agreed that he didn't have much faith in himself and in his ability to successfully make a major change in his life. He said he was going to work on his beliefs, and would get back with me in a few weeks with a list of things he was going to do to help himself with the change. We ended our lunch with a prayer.

I would like to report a happy ending to this story that says that John left the printing business and became a successful poet and musician, but I can't. That happy ending hasn't yet occurred. What actually happened was John continued as the manager of his father's print shop until it finally went out of business several months later. John and his wife are now separated, and John only sees the children on weekends.

Hopefully, John and I will have another lunch together in the near future. I would like to tell John about the great opportunity he now has to use his unique God-given talents in music and poetry. We had prayed for an opportunity to occur, and now it has. I would also like to tell John that when someone is fired from a company, it's the perfect occasion to reevaluate one's direction in life and to reestablish those things that are important. In my opinion, John has been "blessed" with a set of circumstances that can provide both him and his family members with unlimited possibilities for personal growth and self-discovery. The happy ending that John and his family want is just a few beliefs away. As John starts believing more in himself and in his spiritual powers, he can turn his "neutral situations" of losing his job and being separated from his wife and children into "winning situations" of doing the things that make him happy. Happiness comes from doing those things that make you happy.

Happiness comes from doing those things that make you happy.

Doing what makes you happy

Some of you may be wondering why I highlighted such a simple statement as, *Happiness comes from doing those things that make you happy.* You may be thinking that it's such an obvious statement that probably everyone believes it's true. However, the more people I talk to about happiness, the more I wonder if people really do believe this statement. Maybe it's true they understand this statement, but have difficulty understanding a similar statement which says, *Unhappiness comes from doing those things that make you unhappy.* It really doesn't matter where the misunderstanding is. The truth is, many people are trying to find happiness doing things that make them unhappy.

Look at John in the previous story. He's a good example of someone trying to find happiness in an unhappy situation. According to John, he wanted to be happy, yet he was spending most of his time in a print shop doing things in which he had no real interest or skills. John hated his job at the print shop. Is it any wonder that he was so unhappy and frustrated when he finally arrived home after a trying day at the shop? Is it any wonder that his marriage ended up in a legal separation? What made it even more frustrating for John was the fact that he knew exactly what his God-given skills and talents were. He knew his real talents and interest were in the areas of music and poetry. He also knew exactly how he wanted to use his talents. John's problems were that he didn't have enough belief in himself to take control of his life, and he didn't know what steps to take to move from one career to another.

How many of us are living our lives similar to John's? How many of us are spending eight to ten hours a day at a job we have no real interest in? How many of us are so wiped-out at the end of a frustrating day at work that we're unable to adequately handle our parental and marital responsibilities? How many of us are still allowing our parents to control our daily activities? How many of us are controlled by the pursuit of the all-mighty dollar? It's unfortunate, but according to my personal survey, most of us are living our lives in a manner similar to John's.

It's quite obvious that John's story isn't unique. We all have similar shortcomings and unfulfilled dreams. All of us, at one time or another, have had extreme doubts about our abilities and our spiritual powers. All of us, to one degree or another, have had major concerns or fears about unplanned disruptions in our lives. This is normal and is to be expected. But the truth remains, if we don't grab control of our life situations, our life situations will grab control of us. And when this happens, we end up on an emotional roller coaster in which we have little control.

I'm not suggesting we should avoid all things that make us unhappy. There are certain unpleasant tasks such as taking out the evening garbage, filling out income tax forms, and having a tooth drilled that must be done. What I'm suggesting is that each of us thoroughly examine our daily activities in order to determine which events cause us unhappiness, and then do the following. First, eliminate all of the meaningless events that make us unhappy, and second, change our attitudes about the unpleasant events that must be done so they don't cause us unhappiness. Just by changing our attitudes about situations we can have a major influence on our overall happiness. Happiness isn't determined by the situations in our lives, but by our attitudes towards those situations.

Happiness isn't determined by the situations in our lives, but by our attitudes towards those situations.

A Life Changing Ten-Step Program

Do you realize if you don't change a situation, the situation will change by itself? It's true. It's a natural law. The law is called the Law of Change. This law simply says, "Everything in the universe is constantly changing." The great philosophers have stated the law several different ways throughout the centuries. Heraclitus said, "There is nothing permanent except change." A French philosopher said, "Only that which is provisional endures." And I'm sure someone must have said something like, "Every situation in every person's life is temporary." The truth is, we live in a constantly changing universe, and everyone of us has the ability to influence what some of the changes will be.

Few of us are aware of the countless changes that are occurring within us. The changes are happening in such a way that our physical senses can't perceive most of them, but they are occurring. If you have read every lesson in this book up to this page, you have probably changed a great deal. You may not be aware of it, but many changes have probably occurred in your spiritual belief system, as well as in your intellectual understanding of life. This is true even though you may not have agreed with everything you have read. These undetected changes will permit you to do things now that you weren't able to do before. Are you ready to go into action and make major modifications to your life? If you are, expect many changes to occur.

A self-help program has been formulated to help you make the changes you desire. This program, which I recently developed, works extremely well, because it's very spiritual in nature, yet contains many practical and intellectual steps. It's a proven program that my friends and I have used many times. The steps of the program are listed below. This self-help spiritual program is called the *Life Changing Ten-Step Program.*

Step 1:   *In meditation or prayer, tell God about the change you desire in your life. Ask Him if this change interferes with His Will. Listen with your heart for His answer.*

This is a very important step, because it tells God that you have a desire to live your life in accordance with His Will. It's a step in which you surrender your personal will to God.

Step 2:   *In meditation or prayer, ask God to help you overcome all difficulties you are having in forgiving yourself and others.*

In asking God to help you overcome personal difficulties, you're humbly stating that you don't have the personal power to control all aspects of your life and, therefore, need His help.

Step 3:   *Forgive yourself and others for all situations that have blocked the natural flow of love between you and them.*

The importance of forgiveness can't be overstated. Forgiveness is a required step for having prayers and desires materialize. Jesus told us, "You can pray for anything, and if you believe, you can have it. It's yours! But when you are praying, first <u>forgive</u> anyone you are holding a grudge against, so that your Father in Heaven will forgive you of your sins too."

Step 4:   *With the awareness that God is working through your intellect, write down on a sheet of paper the exact change you want to make. Make lists of all the advantages and disadvantages of the change.*

This is a very practical step, as well as a spiritual step. It's practical in that the intellectual skills are providing most of the information. It's a spiritual step, because it's an acknowledgement that God speaks to us through our intellectual minds, as well as through our intuitive feelings.

Step 5: *Review the lists of advantages and disadvantages, and make an intellectual decision. If your intuitive feelings agree with your intellectual decision, it's time to go into action. If the two don't agree, it may be an indication that the intellectual decision is not correct, or that the timing for the change is not right.*

This is the step where the decision is made whether or not to go into action and make the desired change. This step is so important that it has a built-in "check and balance" system. If the intuitive feelings aren't in agreement with the intellectual decision, something is wrong, and the program is temporarily delayed. Either the ego has interfered with an honest appraisal of the situation, and an incorrect decision has been made, or the decision is correct, but the timing of the desired change is wrong. If the intellect and the intuition aren't in agreement, you must return to step #1 and repeat the first five steps.

Step 6: *List on a sheet of paper the events that must occur in order for the desired change to happen. Set measurable, specific goals that will bring about the fulfillment of these required events. Both long-term and short-term, life-enhancing goals should be established.*

The word "event" in this step refers to a significant feat that is much more general than a specific goal. For example, if the desired change is to become an engineer, two probable events would be to determine what type of engineer to become and which college to attend. Some specific goals for the first event would be to write to technical organizations to learn more about engineering, to interview several engineers about their jobs, and to talk to an advisor about required skills. The timing of goals may vary from less than one hour to many years, depending on the change that is desired. Common sense must be used in setting the goals. It's important to be aggressive, yet realistic, in setting meaningful goals.

Step 7:   *Visualize in your mind the exact steps you will take to complete each specific goal. Concentrate on each of the steps for several minutes. Make a collage of images and positive affirmations that illustrate the required actions and the final completion of each goal.*

There are many books on the market today about mind power, mind control, mind imaging, and creative visualization. All of the books that I have read on these subjects lead me to one basic conclusion, that the mind has tremendous powers to bring about physical events. Those of you who practice creative visualization or mind imaging understand exactly what I'm saying. It has been proven by several universities within the United States that picturing in the mind the steps required for a successful completion of an event, prior to that event, greatly enhances one's ability to successfully achieve it. Our minds have extraordinary capabilities that can be unleashed to help us achieve goals.

Step 8:   *Ask God through daily meditations or prayers to help you complete each of the goals. Believe with all your heart that the goals you set will come true. Believing is extremely important.*

Throughout the Bible, we're informed of the importance of believing. Jesus told us, "All things are possible to him that believes." By believing, you're showing God that you have faith in His powers. By believing, you're telling God that you trust His divine love for you. By believing, you're indirectly asking God to use His infinite powers to help you.

Step 9:   *Share your deepest thoughts and feelings about the desired change and the specific goals with one or more intimate, spiritual friends. Ask them to support you in making the change.*

It's very important to have a spiritual support group of one or more loving friends during the time you're making a major change in your life. The purpose of the spiritual support group is to provide a positive, loving environment in which you can safely share your deepest thoughts and feelings without concern of being ridiculed or judged. During a spiritual support group meeting, there is no intellectual advice or information given. The reason spiritual support groups are so powerful is because they help the individuals who are making changes in their lives to believe more in themselves and in their actions. The more the individuals believe, the greater the probability that the desired changes will occur. The Law of Belief says, "What you believe is what you are."

Step 10:   *Go into action with your goals, and expect every-thing to work out perfectly. Start living your life as if the desired change had already occurred. If you expect miracles from God, you will always get them.*

If you have successfully completed the first nine steps of this program, the last step will fall naturally into place. You'll be amazed how effortlessly you'll be able to accomplish your goals. As your spiritual powers are activated, you'll experience many miracles.

The steps of the *Life Changing Ten-Step Program* are listed at the end of this lesson without my personal comments. Because of its spiritual nature, the program will always work no matter what the desired changes are. If you're using another self-help program, such as a modified Alcoholics Anonymous Twelve-Step Program, and it's working for you, I would suggest you continue with it, since it's also a proven spiritual program. However, if you're not actively involved in a life changing program, I would strongly recommend the program presented in this lesson. The *Life Changing Ten-Step Program* is a proven program in which God assists you in making desired changes in your life.

The Life Changing Ten-Step Program is a proven program in which God assists you in making desired changes in your life.

FOLLOW-UP EXERCISES

(1) Make a list of the situations in your life that cause you unhappiness. How many of these situations can be eliminated without too much difficulty? Try to change your attitude about the remaining situations by concentrating on their positive aspects.

(2) Use the *Life Changing Ten-Step Program* in an area of your life that you haven't been able to change to your satisfaction. Be prepared for some pleasant surprises.

Life Changing Ten-Step Program

(1) In meditation or prayer, tell God about the change you desire in your life. Ask Him if this change interferes with His Will. Listen with your heart for His answer.

(2) In meditation or prayer, ask God to help you overcome all difficulties you are having in forgiving yourself and others.

(3) Forgive yourself and others for all situations that have blocked the natural flow of love between you and them.

(4) With the awareness that God is working through your intellect, write down on a sheet of paper the exact change you want to make. Make lists of all the advantages and disadvantages of the change.

(5) Review the lists of advantages and disadvantages, and make an intellectual decision. If your intuitive feelings agree with your intellectual decision, it's time to go into action. If the two don't agree, it may be an indication that the intellectual decision is not correct, or that the timing for the change is not right.

(6) List on a sheet of paper the events that must occur in order for the desired change to happen. Set measurable, specific goals that will bring about the fulfillment of these required events. Both long-term and short-term, life-enhancing goals should be established.

(7) Visualize in your mind the exact steps you will take to complete each specific goal. Concentrate on each of the steps for several minutes. Make a collage of images and positive affirmations that illustrate the required actions and the final completion of each goal.

(8) Ask God through daily meditations or prayers to help you complete each of the goals. Believe with all your heart that the goals you set will come true. Believing is extremely important.

(9) Share your deepest thoughts and feelings about the desired change and the specific goals with one or more intimate, spiritual friends. Ask them to support you in making the change.

(10) Go into action with your goals, and expect everything to work out perfectly. Start living your life as if the desired change had already occurred. If you expect miracles from God, you will always get them.

—Day #15—

Living happily ever after

Remember the fairy tales we used to read as children? Most of them started and finished with the same words. They began with, *"Once upon a time...,"* and they ended with, *"...and they lived happily ever after."* Between those phrases were unique stories filled with adventure, danger, courage, lessons, and love. In most fairy tales, the characters didn't live "happily ever after" until the important lessons in the stories were learned. The same is true about life. Your happiness depends on your willingness to learn the lessons you're here on Earth to learn. You can greatly enhance the learning process by developing a positive attitude.

According to the dictionary, an attitude is a manner of acting, feeling, or thinking that shows one's disposition, mental set, or opinion. Basically, it's the ways we act, feel, and think about situations in our lives. It's a part of our lives in which we have total control. It's also something that is distinctly ours and can't be taken away from us.

Our attitudes determine the amount of happiness we'll experience from any given situation in life. As discussed in an earlier lesson, all situations in life are neutral. There isn't any situation that is good, bad, happy, or sad. Every situation in life is impartial. It's our attitudes about life's experiences that give them meaning. This is extremely important to understand. This means we can influence the amount of happiness we receive from any situation just by changing our attitudes about it. This isn't a new concept. It has been recognized for thousands of years that happiness is not controlled by the situations in our lives, but by our attitudes about the situations.

No one can come along and change your attitude for you. It's impossible. Because your attitude is a direct expression of your essence, it can't be changed by another person. However, it's possible for **you** to make significant changes in your own attitude. You can do this by becoming more knowledgeable about life. By understanding such things as your relationship with God, your spiritual identity, your purpose in life, and your interactions with others, you can make significant changes in your attitude. It has been proven that just by making minor changes in your attitude, you can greatly enhance the overall quality of your life.

By making minor changes in your attitude, you can significantly enhance the overall quality of your life.

An attitude about God

The most important attitude you'll ever develop is your attitude about God. What you believe about God establishes the foundation of your life. Just about everything you think, feel, and do during your lifetime will be a direct or indirect reflection of your attitude about God and your relationship with Him. As an illustration, when a person commits the simple act of stealing paperclips from his employer to avoid spending his own money, he is actually demonstrating that he doesn't trust God and His infinite ability to take care of him. Even if he rationalizes the act of stealing in his mind, he is still breaking one of God's rules (Thou shall not steal.) and expressing a lack of confidence in His protective love.

Your attitude about God often determines the types of emotions you'll experience in life. If you believe that God isn't involved in your daily life and that you aren't protected by His love, you'll live in constant fear. It doesn't matter who you are or how much wealth you have, you'll still live in fear. The fear may be one of not having enough money to adequately live, or the fear of losing the earthly possessions you already have. When you totally believe in God and His protective love, you'll live without fear. I personally believe that God is involved in everything we do. Therefore, every decision I make and every action I take are now done with the knowledge that God is watching over me. Because of my strong belief in God, my fears are very few.

What are your deepest thoughts and feelings about God at this particular moment? Do you believe that there is a God? Do you believe that God is actively involved in your life right now as you read this book? According to recently published information, more than 75% of the world's population believe that a God does exist in one form or another. Of the five billion people living on this planet, over 32% are Christians and believe to one degree or another in the teachings of Jesus Christ. What do you really believe? What is your attitude about God?

In this program, I have presented the following beliefs about God.

- God is a loving Spirit that created and rules the universe. This Spirit is eternal, all-powerful, all-knowing, and infinite.

- God, the Heavenly Father, is a powerful energy force that permeates, penetrates, and/or exists in all things in the universe. God isn't all things, but is in all things.

In the Bible, it says,
- God is a Spirit. (John 4:24)
- God is love. (1 John 4:8)
- Our God is full of compassion. (Psalms 116:5)
- Christ is the Son of God. (Acts 8:37)
- (Christ is) the Son of Man. (Matthew 26:31)
- The Holy Spirit, whom we have received from God, lives within us. (1 Corinthians 6:19)

In the Bible, Jesus said,

- I and my Father are one. (John 10:30)
- It is the Father living in me that is doing the work. Believe me when I say that I am in the Father and the Father is in me. (John 14:10,11)

The statements presented above don't provide a clear picture of God's identity. This is because no one knows exactly who or what God is. Many of us know that He exists, and agree that His Spirit is much greater than what our minds can comprehend. Hopefully, you'll take some time and develop an attitude about God that is based on your most intimate feelings. Your attitude about God and your relationship with Him is the most important one you'll ever develop.

Your attitude about God and your relationship with Him is the most important attitude you'll ever develop.

An attitude about yourself

The second most important attitude to develop is the one you have about yourself. Your thoughts and feelings about such things as who you are, your purpose for living, and your ability to accomplish great tasks have a major influence on your overall happiness. According to the spiritual Law of Thought, what you think about yourself is exactly what you are or quickly becoming. You are today exactly what your thoughts and feelings were about yourself in the past. If you want others to see you in a more positive way, you must first have more positive thoughts and feelings about yourself. Your mind and heart determine who you are and how much happiness you'll have in life.

So how do you feel about yourself right now? How great do you really think you are? How you answer these two questions today will determine how your tomorrows will be. If you have been faithfully involved in this program up to this point, you should have some strong feelings about the following comments. Does your attitude about yourself include these thoughts?

- I am a special child of a loving God.
- I am deeply loved and totally protected at all times by God.
- I am both a human being and a spiritual being.
- My spiritual being is my soul, my primary connection to God.
- My spiritual being is eternal and will return to heaven someday.
- My body is a temporary "vehicle" for my soul and will return to dust.
- My main purpose for living is to make minor corrections in my soul.
- I am the creator of my life and my own creation.
- I am living a life that has been outlined by my soul in a Divine Plan.
- I have the free will to determine most of my actions in life.
- I have limited human powers and skills.
- I have unlimited spiritual powers, when I believe I do.
- My life is controlled by spiritual and natural laws.
- I can change situations in my life by changing my thoughts.
- I can talk to God through prayer and meditation, whenever I desire.

I'm sure that some of you don't agree with all of the above statements. That's fine. The above statements represent my own personal attitude about myself and my life on Earth. Whether or not my thoughts and feelings are 100% accurate is difficult to determine. Nevertheless, what is important to me personally is that I have a well-established attitude about myself that provides me with peace of mind and mental strength. Because of my attitude about myself and my abilities, I have been able to accomplish difficult tasks and overcome personal tragedies. Because of my current beliefs, I'm living a very happy, fulfilling life. The most important ingredient for a healthy attitude is spiritual belief.

The most important ingredient for a healthy attitude is spiritual belief.

An attitude about others

One of the most difficult assignments we have while living on Earth is to love all others regardless of our human perceptions of them. We're to develop a love for everyone that is totally unconditional and, therefore, independent of their actions. Many of us have been able to develop this type of love, but only for special individuals. Probably the best illustration of unconditonal love is a mother's love for a child. The deep maternal love a mother feels for her child isn't normally affected by the child's unacceptable behavior. There may be great disappointment and frustration with the child, but the deep, heartfelt love isn't greatly influenced.

Many people believe the reason a mother's love is so deep for her child is because she subconsciously feels that the child is a part of her. She subconsciously views the child as being a living extension of her life. Similar types of feelings which allow us to view others as part of us, or extensions of us, are important to develop on a conscious level, if we're to love others in the way Jesus asked us to.

In the Bible, we're told that the second most important commandment is to love our neighbors as ourselves. Jesus said,

Love the Lord your God with all your heart, soul, and mind. This is the first and greatest commandmant. The second most important is similar. Love your neighbor as much as you love yourself. All the other commandments and all the demands of the prophets stem from these two laws and are fulfilled if you obey them.

The only way we can truly love our neighbors as we love ourselves is by believing that our neighbors are part of us or extensions of us. It's believing in the "oneness" of the human race. It's understanding that everyone on Earth, including the most innocent children, as well as the most feared international terrorists are all "one." A way of seeing others as a part of us is by taking our lists of self-attitudes and directly applying them to everyone else. When we do this with my list of self-attitudes, we end up with the following statements about others:

- They are special children of our loving God.
- They are deeply loved and totally protected at all times by our God.
- They are both human beings and spiritual beings.
- Their spiritual beings are their souls, their primary connections to God.
- Their spiritual beings are eternal and will return to heaven someday.
- Their bodies are temporary "vehicles" for their souls.
- Their main purpose for living is to make corrections in their souls.
- They are the creators of their lives and their own creations.
- They are living lives that have been outlined in Divine Plans.
- They have the free will to determine most of their actions.
- They have limited human powers and skills.
- They have unlimited spiritual powers, when they believe they do.
- Their lives are controlled by spiritual and natural laws.
- They can change situations in their lives by changing their thoughts.
- They can talk to our God through prayer and meditation.

By understanding that everyone else is a child of God living on Earth to make minor corrections in their eternal soul, it becomes easier to accept them as equals. It becomes easier to perceive them as spiritual brothers and sisters. By understanding that everyone else is spiritually equivalent to us and loved by the same God, it becomes easier to accept their actions and to unconditionally love them.

By understanding that everyone else is spiritually equivalent to us, it becomes easier to accept their actions and to unconditionally love them.

An attitude about life

What are your feelings and thoughts about your life? Are you generally happy about the circumstances in your life, or do you feel that life hasn't been kind to you? Do you view each difficult situation as a problem or as an opportunity to grow? Are you grateful for what you have, or are you discontented with what you don't have? Is your cup of life half-empty or half-full? How you answer these questions says a lot about your overall attitude about life.

If you're not happy in life, I'm sure it shows in your general attitude. I'm sure there are many things you're doing and saying daily that are clear indications of your unhappiness. If you want to change your life and become a happier person, you can do it simply by changing some of your general thoughts about life. The wise philosopher Marcus Aurelius once said, "The happiness of your life depends upon the character of your thoughts."

One way of changing the "character of your thoughts" is by saturating your mind with positive, exciting statements about life. I have personally found that by meditating on certain factual statements, my mind has become more accepting of life's truths. You may find that meditating on the following statements about happiness will help you develop a more positive attitude about life.

- Happiness comes only to those who desire to be happy.
- Happiness is an attitude that comes from within.
- Happiness is a loving relationship with God.
- Happiness is serving God and others.
- Happiness is knowing who you really are.
- Happiness is appreciating what you have.
- Happiness is doing the things that make you happy.
- Happiness is not doing the things that make you unhappy.
- Happiness is fulfilling your Divine Plan.
- Happiness is forgiving all others.
- Happiness is making others happy.
- Happiness is believing in yourself.
- Happiness is a peaceful meditation.
- Happiness is having loving relationships with others.
- Happiness is knowing that you're continuously growing.
- Happiness is knowing that you'll go to heaven someday.
- Happiness is experiencing life as an exciting, spiritual adventure.

What would you add to the above list? I'm sure you have some personal thoughts about what brings happiness. Maybe you would like to make your own list.

Happiness is experiencing life as an exciting, spiritual adventure.

Kiss and White Lily for My Dearest Girl

8

Kiss & White Lily for My Dearest Girl

LATELY, I GET NERVOUS JUST LOOKING AT SHIRAMINE-SAN.

SHIRA-MINE-SAN.

SHIRAMINE-SAN!

U—

UM...!

YES. GOOD-BYE.

ARE YOU OFF TO STUDY IN THE LIBRARY AGAIN TODAY?

GOOD LUCK!

DOKI

DOKI

DOKI (BADMP)

Kiss & White Lily
for My Dearest Girl

8

{CANNO}

I WON'T LET YOU GET AWAY WITH THAT.

...BUT YOU'RE NOT SPYING ON ME, ARE YOU!?

I DON'T MIND IF YOU DO...

NO, I'M NOT!

UH...

...CAN I STUDY WITH YOU?

DOKI

DOKI (BADMP)

DOKI

DOKI

DOKI

I JUST...

MY HEART THROBS.

ZAWA (CLAMOR)

ZAWA

ZAWA

2-A

BUT I STILL WANT TO SPEND TIME WITH HER...

I WONDER IF SOMETHING'S WRONG WITH ME.

Notice of Student Council Elections

6

YOU GOTTA RUN FOR STUDENT COUNCIL PRESIDENT!

SHIRAMINE-SAN!

ばんっ

BAN
(THUD)

WE'LL LOSE OUR CLUB!

IF ONE OF THE CURRENT OFFICERS...LIKE TATSUMI-SAN AND HER GROUP, BECOMES PRESIDENT, NOTHING WILL EVER CHANGE.

...SO YOU'VE SEEN HOW TOUGH THE STUDENT COUNCIL HAS BEEN ON THE LITTLE ONES RECENTLY, RIGHT!?

YOU'VE HELPED WITH A BUNCH OF CLUBS...

I WASN'T REALLY PLANNING TO...WHY?

I WONDER IF THEY'RE HOPING FOR A STUDENT COUNCIL SWITCH UP TOO...

I KNOW THE GARDENING CLUB ONLY GOT A SMALL PLOT TO WORK WITH...

EXACTLY! THAT'S WHY YOU SHOULD DO IT!

BUT... I'M SORRY.

I'M NOT PLANNING ON RUNNING IN THE ELECTION...

YES, BEING ABLE TO HELP PEOPLE DOES MAKE IT A TEMPTING POSITION...

REALLY... NOT YOU TOO...?

I THINK YOU'D MAKE A GOOD STUDENT COUNCIL PRESIDENT.

THEY CAME TO THAT SOLUTION AFTER CAREFULLY CONSIDERING EVERYONE.

EVEN IF THE PRESIDENT CHANGES, IT WON'T—

...BUT THE ROSE GARDEN SITUATION WASN'T JUST AN ARBITRARY DECISION ON THEIR PART, RIGHT?

Note A

I THINK YOU'RE BETTER AT CONSIDERING PEOPLE THAN ANYONE ELSE!

GATA (CLATTER)

TH—

THANK YOU?

YOU MAY EVEN HELP A LOT OF PEOPLE.

YOU COULD EVEN CHANGE THE WHOLE SCHOOL...

...JUST LIKE YOU...

...HELPED ME...

IF YOU'RE INTERESTED, THEN WHY DON'T YOU TRY IT?

I'LL THINK ABOUT IT!

I SAID SOMETHING LIKE THAT TO YOU ONCE TOO, DIDN'T I?

...YOU'RE RIGHT.

BUT THE DEADLINE TO ANNOUNCE YOUR CANDIDACY IS COMING UP SOON.

I'M STILL THINKING ABOUT IT.

IS IT TRUE YOU'RE GOING TO RUN FOR PRESIDENT, SHIRAMINE-SAN!?

SHIRAMINE-SAN...

IT WOULD BE SO AWESOME IF YOU WERE THE PRESIDENT!

WE'RE ROOTING FOR YOU!

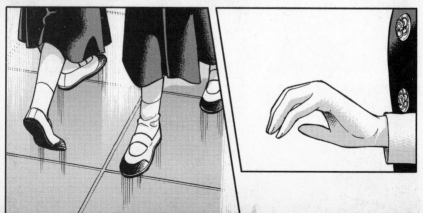

IF I GET TOO CLOSE, MY HEART JUST RACES AND I WON'T BE ABLE TO CALM DOWN.

THIS IS PROBABLY FOR THE BEST...

DO YOU HAVE ANYONE IN MIND TO CAMPAIGN WITH?

AND POSTERS TOO.

IF YOU RUN FOR PRESIDENT, YOU'LL HAVE TO MAKE SPEECHES AND STUFF.

KIIN (DING)

KOON (DONG)

NO... I'M NOT EVEN SURE I'M GOING TO RUN YET.

CHIRA (GLANCE)

KURO-
SAWA-
SAN!

IF YOU HAVEN'T EATEN YET, LET'S HAVE LUNCH TOGETHER!

WHAT ABOUT KUROSAWA-SAN? SHE'S JUST ABOUT AS POPULAR AS YOU.

WHA—?

WOULD SHE ACTUALLY AGREE TO DO IT?

THAT'S NOT REALLY HER THING, IS IT?

THIS MIGHT BE THE FIRST TIME I'VE SPENT MY BREAK IN THE CLASSROOM NEXT DOOR...

KUROSAWA-SAN!

HUH?

THESE ARE FROM CHIHARU!

TRY IT! HAVE SOME!

ぱく

PAKU (MUNCH)

THANKS.

SURE.

IF YOU'RE FREE, CAN YOU HELP US CLEAN UP?

KURO-SAWA-SAN!

I EVEN HAVE FRIENDS NOW.

I'M NOT THE SAME PERSON I USED TO BE.

I'LL BE FINE EVEN IF I'M NOT ALWAYS WITH SHIRAMINE-SAN.

NO... NOT REALLY.

KUROSAWA-SAN? IS SOMETHING WRONG?

SO I WON'T GET LONELY.

SIGN: LIBRARY

図書室

AH.

EXAMS ARE COMING UP SOON.

EVEN THOUGH I'M NOT WATCHING YOU, YOU'RE STILL STUDYING, RIGHT?

YEAH...

...IT FEELS LIKE IT'S BEEN A LONG TIME.

YEAH, IT DOES...

...YOU NEVER STUDY, SO I'LL STILL BE ABLE TO BEAT YOU EASILY!

KYU (GRIP)

EVEN IF I DO BECOME STUDENT COUNCIL PRESIDENT...

...AND I GET EVEN BUSIER THAN I AM NOW...

16

...I SAID SOMETHING TO MOTIVATE YOU ONCE, RIGHT?

I THINK THAT'S GREAT.

AND NOW YOU'RE THE ONE WHO'S MOTIVATING ME...

I'M LEARNING A LOT AND MEETING NEW PEOPLE.

...I'M TALKING TO OUR CLASSMATES MORE THAN USUAL...

BECAUSE OF WHAT'S GOING ON...

......

SO I'M GRATEFUL TO YOU FOR THAT...

I'M...
ROOTING
FOR YOU.

THIS IS WHAT
YOU DECIDED,
SO I BELIEVE
IN IT!

IT'S BEEN A
LONG TIME, SO I
THOUGHT I SHOULD
ABSORB AS MUCH OF
YOU AS I COULD.

WHAT?

......

THAT'S
ENOUGH,
ISN'T IT!?

I HAVE
TO GO.

SHIRA-
MINE-
SAN!

I'M SORRY.

...OKAY.

SEE YOU.

I'M SUPPOSED TO MEET HER TO GET ADVICE.

I HAVE PLANS.

I'VE BEEN INTRODUCED TO A FORMER STUDENT COUNCIL MEMBER...

MAYBE I'VE GOTTEN EVEN WEAKER THAN I USED TO BE.

We will now have registration of the candidates for the student council election and an informational meeting.

All candidates please come to the multipurpose room.

Once again—

KUROSAWA-SAAAN!

LET'S GO CHEER ON SHIRAMINE-SAN!

YEAH...

ZAWA (CLAMOR)

ZAWA

ZAWA

LOOK AT THOSE TWO!

OH!

THAT'S TATSUMI-SAN AND TORAYAMA-SAN.

THE OTHER PRESIDENTIAL CANDIDATES?

YEAH.

THEY'RE BOTH PRETTY POPULAR, SO IT'S GOING TO BE QUITE A RACE!

DOKIN (THROB)

DOKIN

DOKIN

I HAVE TO TELL HER...

"I'M ROOTING FOR YOU.

DOKIN

DOKIN

"YOU CAN DEFINITELY WIN.

"I KNOW BEST HOW AMAZING YOU ARE.

DOKI (BADMP)

SHIRAMINE-SAN!

HEY, KUROSAWA-SAN! DIDJA HEAR!? SHIRAMINE-SAN SAID—

"SO... GOOD LUCK!"

KURO-SAWA-SAN!

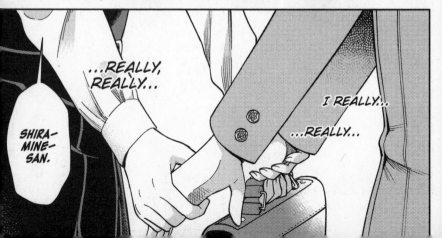

...REALLY, REALLY...

I REALLY...

...REALLY...

SHIRA-MINE-SAN.

WHY?

I DO FEEL BAD ABOUT GETTING EVERYONE'S HOPES UP, THOUGH.

I DECIDED NOT TO.

AND... THERE'S SOMETHING MUCH MORE IMPORTANT TO ME...

...THAN A HUGE GOAL LIKE CHANGING THE SCHOOL.

...BUT I CAN DO THAT WITHOUT JOINING THE STUDENT COUNCIL.

IT WOULD BE NICE TO BE ABLE TO HELP EVERYONE...

I ALMOST LOST SIGHT OF THAT!!

BISHII (POINT)

I'VE DEDICATED MY HIGH SCHOOL LIFE TO DEFEATING YOU!

SOMETHING IMPORTANT...?

YES.

SO, LIKE...

...I DECIDED TO PUT MY PROMISE TO YOU AHEAD OF MY REPUTATION.

I'VE ALREADY DONE ALL THIS WORK CATCHING UP TO YOU.

SABOTAGING MY CHANCE TO WIN IS TOTALLY OUT OF THE QUESTION!

THAT'S ALL.

HEY!

LET GO!

NO.

28

SORRY, SHIRAMINE-SAN.

BUT I'M REALLY HAPPY...

HEY!

I'VE JUST FALLEN IN LOVE WITH HER.

THERE'S NOTHING WRONG WITH ME—

32

I REALLY...

YOU'RE ALWAYS SO UNPREDICT-ABLE!!

GUI (SHOVE)

BUT YOU KEPT AVOIDING ME EARLIER...

FIGURED WHAT OUT?

I FIGURED IT OUT!

I...

GYU (SQUEEZE)

......

YOU CAN'T JUST START SAYING SOMETHING AND THEN NOT FINISH!!

ON SECOND THOUGHT, I'M NOT TELLING!

TA (TROT)

SUZUKI *GO CLUB.*

 TANAKA *MATH CLUB.*

 TAKAHASHI *RAKUGO APPRECIATION SOCIETY.*

Strategy Meeting

I WONDER... IF TATSUMI-SAN'S GONNA BE PRESIDENT.

IT COULD BE TORA-YAMA-SAN.

I REALLY WANTED SHIRAMINE-SAN TO RUN...

Go Club
Shogi Club
Math Club
Rakugo Appreciation Society

YOU'RE A GENIUS!

WHAT ABOUT WE FLIP IT AROUND AND GO GET BUDDY-BUDDY WITH TATSUMI-SAN!?

YEAH!

GACHA (KACHAK)

ALL RIGHT! THIS IS THE PLAN!

GONYO
?

WE'LL FIND HER WEAK SPOT...

WE'LL MAKE IT SO SHE CONSIDERS OUR REQUESTS FIRST...

WE'LL BE HONEY-POTS...

GONYO GONYO (WHISPER)

NOPE...

THIS ISN'T GOING TO WORK, IS IT?

* PEOPLE OTHER THAN THE MAIN CHARACTERS HAVE STORIES TOO. HERE, WE PRESENT THE "LITTLE LOVE" STORIES HAPPENING BEHIND THE SCENES.

RAKUGO: A TRADITIONAL JAPANESE STORYTELLING PERFORMANCE IN WHICH A SINGLE PERFORMER ENTERTAINS THE AUDIENCE WITH A STORY USING JUST THEIR VOICE, A FAN, AND A PIECE OF CLOTH TO PORTRAY MULTIPLE CHARACTERS.

* *Yurine Kurosawa* *

Yurine Kurosawa

Second-year student at Seiran Academy High School. An apparent genius and rival to Ayaka Shiramine. Since she gets results above average even when she's not trying, she can be awkward at times, but her relationship with Shiramine is changing her little by little. She's always been pretty fond of Shiramine, but as she herself changes, the nature of her feelings are changing too.

Chapter 37: *Dragon and Tiger*

JUST UNTIL WE FIND SOMEONE TO ADOPT HER.

OH YEAH, YOU'RE TAKING CARE OF A CAT FOR THE VOLUNTEER CLUB, AREN'T YOU?

SO CUUUTE!!

SHE'S ONLY THREE MONTHS OLD AND SHE'S SUPER-CUTE.

WELL, BOTH ARE ALL ABOUT HELPING.

STILL...ISN'T IT HARD DOING BOTH STUDENT COUNCIL AND VOLUNTEER CLUB?

YOU REALLY ARE THE ONLY CHOICE FOR PRESIDENT!

SO TOUCHED!

YOU'RE JUST SO MUCH MORE CONSIDERATE THAN TATSUMI-SAN!

WE'RE ALL COUNTING ON YOU, TORAYAMA-SAN!!

I WANT TO BE THE STUDENT COUNCIL PRESIDENT.

I'LL PUT UP WITH A WHOLE LOT TO MAKE THAT HAPPEN.

KYU (SQUEAK)

I WANT PEOPLE TO DEPEND ON ME.

I'LL ELIMINATE WHAT STANDS IN MY WAY, EVEN NAGISA TATSUMI!

UGH!!!

N.Tatsumi

?

GIKU

GIKU (CREAK)

IT'S ALL RIGHT! LET'S GET GOING!!

SHAKU

SHAKU (STIFF)

IT'S NOTHING!!

BA (FWIP)

TORAYAMA-SAN? IS SOMETHING WRONG WITH YOUR HANDKER-CHIEF?

GU (CLENCH)

42

EVERYONE... I'M SORRY.

BUT I JUST CAN'T TELL YOU THIS.

ギュ (GYU (GRIP))

N.J.

THAT WAS CLOSE...

NO ONE NOTICED IT.

KYORO (GLANCE)

KYORO

ガチャ (GACHA (KACHAK))

43

HIKARI.

BECAUSE I CAN JUST ASK YOU.

YOU REALLY PISS ME OFF...

I CAN'T TELL YOU...

HIKARIII!

UNDER THE SINK!

IT'S YOUR HOUSE! HOW DO YOU NOT EVEN KNOW THAT!?

WHERE'S THE REFILL FOR THE SHAMPOO?

....

...THAT I'M LIVING WITH HER!!

HER
↓

フシャーッ
FUSHAAA
(HISSS)

グシャ
GUSHA
(CRUMPLE)

YOU DIDN'T SORT THE CLEAN LAUNDRY VERY WELL, DID YOU?

I PANICKED FOR A MOMENT BECAUSE I WAS CARRYING AROUND ONE OF YOUR HANDKER-CHIEFS!

OH...

I MESSED IT UP? SORRY.

...

ぐわ〜
GUWA
(RAWR)

I DO, BUT...

DO YOU EVEN REALIZE YOU CAUSED TROUBLE FOR ME!?

THAT'S ALL!!?

MROW!!

OH YEAH... NAGISA.

IT'S NOT LIKE I ACTUALLY WANT TO LIVE IN HER HOUSE WITH HER.

I'M STAYING WITH HER FAMILY WHILE I'M IN HIGH SCHOOL BECAUSE OF THINGS ON MY PARENTS' END.

...NO ONE ACTUALLY PAYS ATTENTION TO LITTLE THINGS LIKE THAT, YOU KNOW.

IRAAA (GRRR)

WORRYING ABOUT IT ISN'T WORTH IT.

GUI GUI (PUSH)

AND YOU'RE JUST TOO LAZY!!

GYA

YOU'RE JUST NITPICKING.

AND WHAT IF SOMEONE FINDS OUT BECAUSE OF A LITTLE SLIPUP LIKE THAT!?

GYA (GRIPE)

GYA

I WAS ROOTING FOR HER BECAUSE SHE'S NOTHING LIKE TATSUMI-SAN!

MAYBE THEY'RE ACTUALLY REALLY CLOSE FRIENDS?

THOSE TWO ARE COLLABORAT- ING BEHIND OUR BACKS.

IF ANYONE... SAW US LIKE THIS...

46

TA-TSUMI-SAN...

I'LL MAKE SURE MY LIFE IS ABSOLUTELY PERFECT AND NO ONE FINDS OUT— NO MATTER WHAT!!!

LET'S VOTE FOR SOMEONE ELSE...

THAT CAN'T HAPPEN!!!

AHHHHH!

WHAT SORT? SHOW US SOME PICS!

OHHH!

I TOOK ONE IN FOR THE VOLUNTEER CLUB JUST RECENTLY.

DO YOU HAVE A CAT?

IS THAT CAT HAIR?

I'LL GET IT FOR YOU!

...THERE'S A WHITE HAIR ON YOUR UNIFORM.

AH... SHE'S A WHITE KITTEN, ONLY THREE MONTHS OLD...

OH YEAH... YOU HAVE A CAT TOO, RIGHT, TORAYAMA-SAN...?

TATSUMI-SAN COMES OFF AS COLD, SO I REALLY DIDN'T THINK SHE'D BE INTERESTED IN ANIMALS...

SHE HAS A CAT.

IT WAS THE VOLUNTEER CLUB. DIDN'T YOU KNOW THAT?

UGH...

DIDN'T SHE SAY SHE TOOK HER IN FOR A CLUB...?

Y-YEAH! WHAT A COINCI- DENCE!

!?

I'VE SEEN TORAYAMA-SAN WITH WHITE CAT HAIR ON HER CLOTHES TOO, YOU KNOW...

WHA !?

IT'S A THREE- MONTH- OLD WHITE KITTEN...

WHA

AAI?

IT'S JUST A COINCIDENCE.

NO ONE WILL BELIEVE THAT!!!

THEY'RE ALL FROM THE SAME LITTER, SO THEY LOOK REALLY SIMILAR, DON'T THEY!!?

AND THAT STYLE*COUCH IS REALLY NICE, ISN'T IT!!?

KOKU (NOD)

KOKU

THE VOLUNTEER CLUB HAD THREE OF THEM, RIGHT!?

TATSUMI, YOU TOOK IN A KITTEN TOO, HUH!?

LIE

T—

COINCI-DENCE... COINCI-DENCE...

OH, SO THAT'S HOW IT IS!

NO ENTRANCE

カチャ…

KACHA (KCHAK)

50

...I'LL ADMIT THAT I UNDER-ESTIMATED.

ぱさっ POSA (PLOP)

Caran Block

I'M SORRY...

I DIDN'T THINK THEY'D COMPARE STORIES BEHIND THE SCENES LIKE THAT.

YOU HAVE TO BE MORE CAREFUL ABOUT WHAT YOU SAY!

I THOUGHT WE WERE DONE FOR!!

WE WERE SAVED BECAUSE EVERY-ONE'S GUILLIBLE...

NO ENTRAN

I DON'T WANT ANYONE GETTING THE IDEA WE'RE ACTUALLY FRIENDS OR ANYTHING!

I MIND IT!

BUT...WHY DO WE NEED TO HIDE IT IN THE FIRST PLACE?

IT'S NOT LIKE WE'RE DOING ANYTHING WRONG.

ISN'T IT JUST WASTED EFFORT?

WELL... YEAH, BUT...

YOU ACT ALL COOL AT SCHOOL, BUT AT HOME YOU'RE A MESS.

WHAT ABOUT YOUR REPUTATION?

MY REP-UTATION? I DON'T REALLY CARE...

SO FROM NOW ON YOU HAVE TO BE MORE CAREFUL!

MUNI (SQUISH)

IT'S ALL BECAUSE YOU'RE SO CARELESS!!

GYAN

NO ENTRANCE

THAT DOESN'T HAVE ANYTHING TO DO WITH THIS...

GYAN

AND THE FAUCET TOO!!

YOU HAVE TO TURN OFF THE LIGHTS WHEN YOU'RE DONE IN A ROOM!

MUNIII

SINCE I HAVE YOU, LET'S GET SOME STUFF STRAIGHT...

BESIDES!

YOU'RE ALWAYS SO SLOPPY WITH STUFF...!!

THERE'S SOMEONE UP ON THE ROOF.

GYAN

SENSEI!!

GYAN (GRIPE)

52

IS SOMEONE UP HERE?

カチャ...
KACHA
(KACHAK)

WE LIVE TOGETHER, SO IT ALL ENDS UP FALLING ON ME—

MAKE SURE YOU LOCK BACK UP WHEN YOU'RE DONE.

パタン
PATAN
(SHUT)

SORRY... I'M USING THIS SPACE TO PRACTICE MY SPEECH.

...THIS IS BECAUSE YOU NEVER SHUT UP.

I THOUGHT YOU DIDN'T WANT ANYONE TO FIND OUT...

OKAY!

SO THAT'S WHAT IT IS.

SIGN: STUDENT COUNCIL ROOM

生徒会室

SHE REALLY PISSES ME OFF!!!

CAN I HAVE PERMISSION TO MAKE SOME COPIES?

I WANTED TO TALK ABOUT THE ELECTION PUBLICITY PAPER...

I ALREADY TURNED IN MY SUBMISSION, DIDN'T I?

ARMBAND: PUBLICITY

WHAT IS IT?

IS TORAYAMA-SAN HERE?

GARA (SLIDE)

...ABOUT THOSE RUMORS GOING AROUND...

R-RUMORS ...?

?

THERE AREN'T ANY PROBLEMS WITH THAT, BUT...

IF IT IS TRUE, THEN I WOULD LOVE TO PUT IT IN THE ELECTION INFO!

WHAAA—?

THEY'RE SAYING YOU AND TATSUMI-SAN LIVE TOGETHER...

...I HAD NO IDEA SUCH A RUMOR WAS GOING AROUND.

SO?

54

BUT WHEN I HEARD THAT RUMOR...

...FOR PEOPLE WHO DON'T KNOW EITHER OF YOU TO APPROACH YOU...

IT'S KIND OF HARD...

...YOU SUDDENLY FELT MORE APPROACH-ABLE!

...S-SAY THIS RUMOR IS TRUE...

...WHO WOULD ACTUALLY BE HAPPY ABOUT IT?

I THINK IT WOULD BE GOOD FOR BOTH OF YOUR REPUTA-TIONS.

WHAT DO YOU SAY?

SHE HAS A POINT...

IT'LL BE EASIER FOR UNDERCLASS-MEN TO VOTE FOR PEOPLE IF THEY FEEL FAMILIAR.

ON THE OTHER HAND, NAGISA ACTS SO COOL...

......

I'M SO DISAPPOINTED.

I CAN'T BELIEVE SHE'S ACTUALLY SO PATHETIC.

I'M THE TYPE WHO TAKES CARE OF PEOPLE.

SEEING HOW I REALLY AM ISN'T GOING TO MAKE PEOPLE THINK LESS OF ME, NOW IS IT?

SHE'S EVEN PERFECT AT HOME!

AMAZING!

I TOLD HER!!

...BUT, YOU KNOW... I CAN'T REACH...

PON (PAT)

THIS STRATEGY IS ONLY NATURAL!

I'VE BEEN TOO NICE!!

BRING IT BACK TO MY DESK WHEN YOU'RE DONE.

YOU'RE WELL PREPARED...

HUH?

...THANKS...

WANT THIS?

WELL, SORRY FOR NOT CONSIDERING THAT!

BECAUSE I TAKE INTO ACCOUNT HOW TALL I AM.

...BUT IS SHE REALLY SO BAD THAT I HAVE TO DRAG HER THROUGH THE MUD?

...SHE'S NOT A GOOD PERSON...

...MAYBE I WENT TOO FAR...

...I JUST TOLD THE TRUTH!!

I JUST USED IT IN ORDER TO WIN!!

CAN YOU DOUBLE-CHECK THE ELECTION PUBLICITY PAPER?

GARA (SLIDE)

58

SHOW US TOO!

TORA-YAMA-SAN!

Candid Look at Our Candidates for

A behind-the-scenes feature on Tatsumi-san and Torayama-san!

Do they get along at home? What's it like ro

Torayama...

THANKS.

IF IT'S ALL OKAY, THEN WE'LL BE DISTRIBUTING THEM ON MONDAY.

ARMBAND: PUBLICITY

TATSUMI-SAN'S NOT HERE?

HUH?

I WENT AND TOLD EVERYONE ABOUT HOW MESSY NAGISA CAN BE...

IS IT REALLY RIGHT TO WIN THE ELECTION THAT WAY?

NAGISA AND I MAY NOT GET ALONG...

TELL HER TO STOP BY THE PUBLIC RELATIONS ROOM LATER.

IS THIS... REALLY OKAY?

...WE REALLY WANTED TO INCLUDE THAT...

B— BUT...

I THINK IT WILL BE REALLY GOOD FOR YOU.

YOU'LL GET SO MANY MORE SUPPORTERS AFTER PEOPLE SEE THIS.

TAKING IT OUT COULD PUT THE PRESIDENCY OUT OF YOUR REACH...!

SIGN: PUBLIC RELATIONS COMMITTEE

広報委員会

IT MIGHT EVEN GAIN ME SUPPORT...

...AND GET ME ELECTED.

...YOU'RE RIGHT. IF PEOPLE READ THIS ARTICLE...

...IT PROBABLY WON'T HURT ME IN ANY WAY.

BUT... MORE THAN ALL THAT...

THAT'S RIGHT! SO...

AND MAYBE WHEN IT GETS OUT THAT I HAD IT CANCELED...

...PEOPLE WILL SEE ME AS INCONSISTENT.

...I WANT TO MAKE CHOICES THAT I CAN LIVE WITH.

広報委員会

63

I WAS TOLD THAT I NEEDED TO DOUBLE-CHECK THE ELECTION PUBLICITY PAPER...

HAVE I INTERRUPTED SOMETHING?

NO...WE NEED TO MAKE SOME CHANGES...

...SO I'LL BRING IT BY AGAIN TOMORROW.

YOU WROTE SOME NICE-SOUNDING STUFF IN HERE.

DO YOU REALIZE HOW MUCH YOU SOUND LIKE A VILLAIN RIGHT NOW...?

THAT'S BECAUSE I'M CONFIDENT I WON'T LOSE.

IF YOU READ IT CLOSELY, IT SAYS YOU'RE GOING TO BE TOUGH ON ALL THE SMALL CLUBS.

AND YOU DID YOUR USUAL THING.

PYOIN (CHOP)

ぴょいん

AND WE PROBABLY NEVER WILL EITHER.

NAGISA AND I JUST DON'T GET ALONG.

HAA (SIGH)

はあ..

BUT I DON'T THINK IT WOULD BE SO BAD IF OUR RELATIONSHIP CONTINUED LIKE THIS.

Opposites Here Too

SUDOU HIGH SCHOOL SECOND-YEAR. TEAM TATSUMI.

IIDA HIGH SCHOOL SECOND-YEAR. TEAM TORAYAMA.

* Hikari Torayama *

Hikari Torayama

Second-year student at Seiran Academy High School. Current secretary and candidate for next president of the student council. Rival to Nagisa Tatsumi. She's kind and does well with people, but she tends to try to be everything to everyone. Her mother and Nagisa's mother are friends, so she's known Nagisa for a while, but they don't get along. Because of her parents' work, she's living at the Tatsumi household. She's a natural caretaker, so she just ends up looking after Nagisa by default. She's an only child.

EACH CANDIDATE WILL MAKE HER FINAL SPEECH TO THE SCHOOL DURING HOMEROOM NEXT WEEK...

...AND THEN WE WILL ALL VOTE.

AND THAT'S THE SCHEDULE FOR STUDENT COUNCIL ELECTIONS.

ANY QUESTIONS?

Student Council Election
Election Day Schedule
15:00~ Candidates' speeches broadcast to the entire school.
15:15~ Voting in classrooms.
16:00~ Ballots counted.
☆The results will be announced the next day.

ARMBAND: ELECTION COMMITTEE

KAAN (DANG)

2 - C

SEE YOU TOMOR-ROW!

LET'S GO TO THE CLUB MEET-ING!

KOON

KIIN (DING)

KOON (DONG)

...THINK ABOUT WHO YOU WANT TO REPRESENT YOU BEFORE NEXT WEEK COMES.

IF NOT... THEN PLEASE...

YOU DECIDED YET?

HAVE YOU FINISHED WRITING YOUR SPEECH YET?

THE ELECTION'S ALMOST HERE, TATSUMI-SAN!

OH YEAH, SHE STUDIED ABROAD, DIDN'T SHE?

SHE EVEN MADE A SPEECH IN ENGLISH ONCE!

IT WAS JUST FOR A SHORT TIME, THOUGH...

SHE'S ALREADY USED TO THAT.

YOU'RE NOT NERVOUS ABOUT IT BEING BROAD-CAST, ARE YOU?

CALLIGRAPHY

ENGLISH

ABACUS

SWIMMING

I STILL HAD TIME RESERVED FOR OTHER PEOPLE, THOUGH.

...SO I GOT TO DO PRETTY MUCH EVERY-THING.

MY FAMILY IS RELATIVELY WELL OFF...

...I'M *SUPPOSED* TO DO MY BEST TO HELP EVERYONE!

GROWING UP AS FORTUNATE AS I DID...

72

Chapter 38: *Seiran Academy High School Student Council Elections*

IT STARTED BACK IN MY THIRD YEAR OF MIDDLE SCHOOL.

HIKARI TORAYAMA?

CARTON: SOYBEAN COLA

I THINK SO...

MOYA (HAZY)

MOYA

SHE'S IN THE CLASS NEXT TO YOURS, ISN'T SHE?

DON'T LAZE AROUND IN YOUR UNDERWEAR!

!?

ガバッ

GABA (JUMP)

SHE'S GOING TO COME STAY WITH US.

I SPENT SOME TIME WITH HIKARI-CHAN'S MOTHER TODAY.

OUR MOMS ARE FRIENDS ...?

BACK THEN

NO, I DID.

I CLIMBED HIGHER THAN YOU!

HIKARI TORAYAMA!

ALL I REMEMBER IS WE DIDN'T GET ALONG...

ACTUALLY, I THINK I HAD SUCH A BAD IMPRESSION OF HER THAT I COMPLETELY WIPED HER FROM MEMORY.

HEY!!

BESIDES, AREN'T YOU LONELY WITH DAD LIVING ELSEWHERE FOR WORK?

YOU'RE THE ONE WHO'S LONELY, MOM.

HER PARENTS WILL BE AWAY FOR A WHILE FOR WORK...

...AND THEY'D RATHER SHE STAY WITH SOMEONE THEY KNOW THAN MOVE INTO THE DORMS.

OH? WELL, SHE CAN COME STAY WITH US.

THAT WOULD BE WONDERFUL!

I CAN'T ...

NOW

ANYWAY!

IGNORE

SHE'LL BE MOVING IN IN APRIL!

BE NICE TO HER.

I'LL JUST HAVE TO AVOID HER.

...THANK YOU FOR HAVING ME.

W-WELL, IT'S NOT LIKE IT'S GOING TO BE JUST THE TWO OF US...

S-SO?

...BUT HE DID BREAK HIS ARM.

HE'S OKAY...

Mom

HUH...?

DAD GOT IN AN ACCIDENT!?

HUH...?

SO I'M GOING TO BE STAYING HERE A LITTLE BIT LONGER.

WHAT ABOUT ME...?

THERE'S NO WAY!!!

YOU'LL BE STAYING THERE WITH HIKARI-CHAN.

Mom

I REALLY DON'T WANT EVERYONE KNOWING ABOUT IT!!

I HAVE MY OWN STUFF TO DEAL WITH!

PEOPLE ARE GONNA FIND OUT EVENTUALLY, YOU KNOW. WE SHOULD JUST TELL EVERYONE ABOUT IT NOW INSTEAD.

YOU WANNA HIDE THAT WE'RE LIVING TOGETHER...?

GIRI GIRI GIRI GIRI GIRI (GRIND) GIRI

OH.

HEY!

MOM, DAD, PLEASE JUST COME BACK SOON...

HIKARI AND I REALLY DON'T GET ALONG.

GOOD LUCK, TATSUMI-SAN!

THANKS...

HMPH!

UGH...

EVERYTHING AFTER HIGH SCHOOL IS ALREADY SETTLED...

...SO I THOUGHT I'D STOP BY TO CHEER ON MY KOUHAIS BEFORE THEIR BIG ELECTION!

IT'S THE FORMER CLASS PRESIDENT.

SENPAI!

THAT'S RIGHT.

YOU DON'T HAVE TO BE AT SCHOOL RIGHT NOW, DO YOU...?

YEAH, YEAH, THAT'S GOOD!

I'LL BE SURE TO PROPERLY CARRY ON THE WORK THAT YOU WERE DOING.

DON'T WORRY ABOUT IT.

I AM THE ONE WHO DRAGGED BOTH OF YOU ONTO THE STUDENT COUNCIL, AFTER ALL.

I WISH SHE CAME TO SEE JUST ME...

OF COURSE I WILL!

YOU'LL CHEER ME ON, WON'T YOU?

BUT I ACTUALLY LISTEN TO WHAT THE OTHER STUDENTS WANT! AND I HAVE A LOT OF SUPPORT.

BUT YOU'RE BOTH SUPER TALENTED...

...SO I CAN'T CHOOSE!

I DON'T GET A VOTE EITHER.

NOT ANYMORE.

WHY DOES EVERYONE ALWAYS PUT HIKARI AND ME ON THE SAME LEVEL!?

AND I'M PRETTY SURE PEOPLE TRUST ME MORE TOO.

I HAVE BETTER GRADES!

I'M SURE I'M MUCH BETTER...

Hikari Hiiyama 97

Tatsumi 98

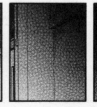

HEY, HAVE YOU DECIDED WHO YOU'RE GOING TO VOTE FOR FOR STUDENT COUNCIL?

ばったり。
BATTARI
(BABAM)

OH!

TATSUMI-SAN'S JUST KIND OF SCARY...

I THINK TORAYAMA-SAN FOR PRESIDENT.

WHY?

MY CLUB IS TOTALLY TEAM TORAYAMA...

I'M GOING TO VOTE FOR TORAYAMA-SAN!

I JUST WONDER, WHY...

NO... I'M USED TO IT.

TATSUMI-SAN! THAT'S SO NOT TRUE!!

I OWE TORAYAMA-SAN A LOT.

IT'S A COINCIDENCE! IT'S JUST A COINCIDENCE, TATSUMI-SAN!!

NO... I DON'T THINK I CAN AFFORD TO IGNORE THIS.

I NEED TO CONSIDER HOW THIS HAPPENED.

FIGURE OUT WHAT CHARM TORAYAMA HAS THAT I DON'T...

W-WE'LL THINK ABOUT IT TOO!!

WHY DOES EVERYONE ALWAYS PREFER HIKARI...!?

TORA-YAMA-SAN...

I THINK I'LL VOTE FOR TORA-YAMA-SAN.

HISO (PSST)

AWW! BUT THEN SHE'LL...

BECAUSE SHE LOST...

SHE WON'T BE ABLE TO STAY ON THE STUDENT COUNCIL, WILL SHE?

...WHAT'LL HAPPEN IF SHE LOSES?

HEY...I WAS JUST THINKING...

SHH!

KEEP IT DOWN!

GAMI (SNARL)

GAMI

AND YOU SHOULD TRY PAYING MORE ATTENTION TO OTHERS!

YOU'RE ALWAYS TRYING TO BE EVERYONE'S FRIEND!

JUST THINKING ABOUT IT MAKES ME MAD.

THAT'S WHY PEOPLE HAVE A GOOD IMPRESSION OF HER...?

IS IT HOW SHE PRIORITIZES THE LITTLE CLUBS?

THE DIFFERENCE BETWEEN HIKARI AND ME...

DID SHE ALWAYS HAVE A MOLE THERE?

I'VE NEVER LOOKED AT HER THIS MUCH BEFORE...

THAT WAS HOW WE WERE WHEN WE STARTED LIVING TOGETHER...

FINE! WELL, DON'T YOU INVADE MY SPACE EITHER.

DON'T YOU DARE CROSS THIS LINE!

I'LL DO IT TOMORROW.

WHAT'S HER DEAL? ALWAYS TAKING CARE OF EVERYTHING.

BAN (SLAM)

DIDN'T I TELL YOU TO PUT YOUR CLEAN CLOTHES AWAY IN YOUR OWN ROOM!?

HONESTLY, NAGISA!

SHE'S KIND...

OR RATHER, SHE'S GOOD AT TAKING CARE OF PEOPLE.

OH, FINE...

MAYBE SHE'S JUST A GOOD PERSON?

PEOPLE DON'T NORMALLY TAKE CARE OF SOMEONE THEY ALWAYS FIGHT WITH.

...HM?

SHIRT: T-SHIRT

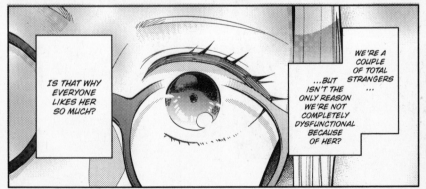

IS THAT WHY EVERYONE LIKES HER SO MUCH?

WE'RE A COUPLE OF TOTAL STRANGERS...

...BUT ISN'T THE ONLY REASON WE'RE NOT COMPLETELY DYSFUNCTIONAL BECAUSE OF HER?

84

I WANT TO KNOW MORE...

...ABOUT...

HIKA...

HON-ESTLY!

IF ONLY I COULD TELL EVERYONE WHAT YOU'RE REALLY LIKE...

THERE'S NO WAY WE CAN PUT SOMEONE IN CHARGE OF THE STUDENT COUNCIL WHO CAN'T EVEN TAKE CARE OF HERSELF!

WHAT IN THE WORLD IS HIKARI TORAYAMA...

...TO ME!?

NO, I REALLY DON'T LIKE HER...

...LIKE THAT?

...BUT YOUR ARROGANCE IS TOTALLY SHOWING.

IT'S GOOD THAT YOU'RE BEING HONEST...

SHE'S ONE TO TALK.

I WONDER WHAT HIKARI WOULD SAY ABOUT THIS PART?

IN THAT CASE, I SHOULD CHANGE THE WORDING.

COME TO THINK OF IT, I'M ALWAYS DOING THAT.

......

I KEEP THINKING ABOUT HIKARI.

IF I WERE HIKARI, THIS WOULD...

IF I WERE HIKARI...

KASA (RUSTLE)

KOSO (PSST)

...So...did you come up with a way to take down Torayama-san?

IT'S ALMOST TIME...

GOOD LUCK, TATSUMI-SAN!

BUT...

UNFORTU-NATELY... I DIDN'T MANAGE TO DO THAT.

SO I'LL HAVE TO FIGHT USING THAT...

...I THINK WHAT I HAVE THAT TORAYAMA LACKS...

...IS HONESTY.

放送室

OKAY... PLEASE MAKE YOUR FINAL SPEECHES BEFORE THE VOTES ARE CAST.

ARE YOU NERVOUS?

I'M NOT...

THANK YOU FOR YOUR HELP TOO.

AND THANK YOU.

GOKURI (GULP)

...I'VE BEEN OBSERVING YOU FOR THE PAST FEW DAYS...

...AND I HAVE SOME THOUGHTS.

WHY DO PEOPLE ALWAYS PIN YOU AS MY RIVAL...?

THERE'S SOMETHING THAT'S BEEN BOTHERING ME.

LET'S REHEARSE BEFORE WE BROADCAST TO THE ENTIRE SCHOOL.

I'LL GO OFF AIR FOR A BIT, THEN.

EXCUSE YOU...

I'M WAY MORE TALENTED THAN YOU, AFTER ALL.

SURE, BUT IT IS JUST A TEST.

C-CAN I TRY TALKING A BIT TOO?

I UNDERSTAND WHY PEOPLE LIKE YOU.

YOU'RE RELIABLE AND KIND.

YOU TAKE CARE OF PEOPLE.

BUT THE REASON EVERYONE SUPPORTS YOU...

...IS BECAUSE YOU'RE JUST THAT CHARMING.

SO LET'S DO THIS FAIR AND SQUARE.

I'M SURE THINGS WILL GO WELL THAT WAY.

IT'S JUST THAT IF YOU'RE NOT IN PEAK FORM, THAT WILL THROW ME OFF TOO.

NOTHING.

...WHAT ARE YOU PLOTTING?

WHA

HUH!?

(GATA) (CLATTER)

92

WE'VE BEEN BROADCASTING LIVE...?

TATSUMI-SAN...

HUH? THE WHOLE SCHOOL?

BROADCASTING TO THE WHOLE SCHOOL...?

SHE ACTUALLY SAID SOMETHING LIKE THAT...?

THE WHOLE SCHOOL!!

...PRETTY MUCH ALL OF IT, I THINK...

LIVE TO THE ENTIRE SCHOOL...

SINCE WHEN, AND FOR HOW LONG...?

CONGRAT-ULATIONS, TATSUMI-SAN!

PAN (POP)

SASH: CONGRATULATIONS

BUT A LOT OF IT WAS BECAUSE OF HOW HARD YOU WORKED TOO!!

I'M NOT SURE HOW I FEEL. IT'S ALMOST LIKE I PLAYED DIRTY...

YOU PROBABLY GAINED A LOT OF SUPPORT FOR THAT STUFF YOU SAID BEFORE THE SPEECHES.

THEY HAVEN'T FINALIZED THE TALLY, BUT I THINK YOU MANAGED TO EKE OUT A WIN.

LET'S GO CHECK IT OUT.

THEY HAVE THE OTHER RESULTS NOW TOO.

I BOUGHT SOME SNACKS AND DRINKS.

ABOUT THAT!

WORK HARD... DO MY PART TOO.

CONGRATS.

THE ELECTION WAS FAIR. A LOSS IS A LOSS.

THE VICE PRESIDENT SPOT IS OPEN, YOU KNOW.

...NOT THAT I ACTUALLY LIKE YOU, OF COURSE.

TOTALLY DIFFERENT THINGS.

BUT... FINE.

SOMETHING WRONG?

I FIGURED YOU'D SAY THAT.

I DON'T LIKE THE THOUGHT OF SETTLING FOR THE VICE PRESIDENCY.

PESHI (SMACK)

I CAN'T STAND YOU...

...BUT I'LL STAY BY YOUR SIDE.

...YOU'RE THE STAR RIGHT NOW.

WHAT ARE YOU DOING HERE IN THE CORNER?

WAI (CHATTER)

WAI

WAI

WAI

YAAAAY!

BUT I CARE!

THEY'RE IGNORING PARTY LINES AND JUST CELEBRATING.

NO ONE CARES ABOUT THAT.

THANKS.

SO THAT'S HOW IT IS...

THAT MAKES THIS—

HUH?

THAT'S THE ONE I WAS DRINKING.

HAAH...

AN INDIRECT KISS...

I DON'T ACTUALLY LIKE HER...

...RIGHT?

WHAT? DON'T STARE AT ME LIKE THAT.

IT DOESN'T BOTHER HER?

HUH ...?

HASE
FORMER PRESIDENT. A SECRETARY BACK THEN.

 SOEJIMA
FORMER VICE PRESIDENT. A HIGH SCHOOL SECOND-YEAR BACK THEN.

 AIZAWA
FORMER TREASURER. ALWAYS PRACTICAL, EVEN BACK THEN.

A Year and a Half Earlier

DON
(THUD)

WOULD YOU STOP RANDOMLY DECIDING TO ADD PEOPLE?

COULD YOU QUIT CAUSING MORE PROBLEMS AFTER THINGS HAVE ALREADY GONE WRONG!?

WE ALREADY HAVE TWO PROBLEMS TO DEAL WITH HERE...

I WONDER.

WHO COULD THAT BE?

THOSE TWO JUST HAPPENED TO BE GOOD CHOICES!

BUT TORAYAMA-CHAN AND TATSUMI-CHAN ARE BOTH HARD WORKERS, AREN'T THEY?

AHHH, SHE'S SO EASY!!

...BUT I'LL HAVE TO DO YOUR WORK TOO.

YOU KNOW.

ぎゅ GYU (SQUEEZE) っ♡

RIGHT! ♡ WE'RE COUNTING ON YOU! ♡

Awww! ♡ BUT WE HAVE A SUPER-TALENTED TREASURER-TO-BE RIGHT HERE!

KISS THEATER: WHAT'S BEHIND THE STORY!? ✳ PEOPLE OTHER THAN THE MAIN CHARACTERS HAVE STORIES TOO. HERE, WE PRESENT THE "LITTLE LOVE" STORIES HAPPENING BEHIND THE SCENES.

Nagisa Tatsumi

Second-year student at Seiran Academy High School. Former secretary and new student council president. Hikari Torayama's rival. She comes off as cool and collected, but she's actually very scattered. She doesn't get along well with Hikari, but she's brushed it off as their personalities just don't mesh. She doesn't really mind having Hikari taking care of her that much. Her family consists of her mom, dad, and an older brother in college.

YOU ASKED ME THAT YESTER...

...DAY...

HEY, HIKARI, WHERE DID YOU PUT LAST MONTH'S MINUTES?

SIGN: STUDENT COUNCIL ROOM

I JUST ORGANIZED ALL OF THAT!!

GOCHAAAAA (MESSY)

HEY!!

SENSEI!?

JUST A MOMENT!!

BA (WHOOSH)

I NEED TO TALK TO HER ABOUT THE GRADUATION CEREMONY...

IS TATSUMI-SAN THERE?

GO (RUMBLE)

HURRY UP AND START CLEANING!!

...mers of the student council ele...
...ollows:

Election Committee
Committee chair: Yumiko Kazama

President: Nagisa Tatsumi   2-C
ce President: Hikari Tora...

Badminton Team

Chapter 39: *Diverging Days*

ARMBANDS: STUDENT COUNCIL

KIRI
(SHARP)

HERE YOU GO.

...SO THIS IS THE PROGRAM FOR GRADUATION.

BUT YOU DON'T ORGANIZE IT!!

YOU'RE SO BAD AT CLEANING!!

DON'T GLARE AT ME LIKE THAT. I ALWAYS PUT EVERYTHING BACK.

PATAN
(SHUT)
ぱたん...

I'LL HAVE SOMEONE THERE WITH ME, WON'T I?

IT'S NOT LIKE SENPAI EVER GOT MAD AT ME FOR THAT. IT'S NOT A PROBLEM.

KATAN
(CLATTER)
カタン

WHAT ARE YOU GOING TO DO WHEN YOU'RE ON YOUR OWN?

I KNOW.

I'M COUNTING ON YOU.

I'M NOT THE LEAST INTERESTED IN YOU AS A PERSON!

...YOU KNOW I'M ONLY HERE AS THE VICE PRESIDENT, RIGHT!?

I'LL HAVE A RED BEAN SODA.

GARA (RATTLE)

...I'M GOING TO GET A DRINK!!

WE DON'T EVEN TALK TO EACH OTHER IN THE CLASSROOM OR IN PASSING...!!

WHAT IS WITH HER? IS SHE TRYING TO PUSH HER LUCK!?

THEY KEEP ALL THESE WEIRD DRINKS IN THE VENDING MACHINES BECAUSE SHE KEEPS BUYING THEM.

GAKON (THUNK)

WELL... I'M GETTING USED TO IT.

HOW ARE THINGS GOING AS VICE PRESIDENT?

TORA-YAMA-SAN.

I SEE.

GAN (SHOCK)

HUH!?

IT SEEMS YOU AND TATSUMI-SAN ARE GETTING ALONG BETTER NOW. THAT'S A RELIEF.

PORO (DROP)

SIGN: STUDENT COUNCIL ROOM

THE OTHER STUDENTS ARE ALL SAYING THAT IT'S A GOOD THING HOW YOU TWO HIT IT OFF AS WELL.

I-IT LOOKS LIKE WE'RE FRIENDS...!?

WAS I WRONG?

RELUCTANT 不本意

!?

生徒会室

PASA
(RUSTLE)

...WE'RE GOOD FRIENDS!!

EVERY-ONE SEEMS TO THINK...

BAN
(THUD)

WHY WOULD THEY THINK THAT!?

I BET THEY DO.

I...

...AND... BECAUSE OF THAT STUFF BEFORE THE FINAL SPEECHES...

PROB-ABLY... BECAUSE I RECOMMENDED YOU FOR VICE PRESIDENT...

I GUESS THAT CAN'T BE HELPED...

AH!

I JUST CAN'T ACCEPT THE SORT OF PERSON YOU ARE...

BUT IT'S NOT TRUE!!

BESIDES, IT'S NOT LIKE THERE'S ANYTHING BAD ABOUT US LOOKING FRIENDLY.

ばん!
BAN

ぱさ
PASA

THEN SHOW ME THE PAPERS FOR THE GRADUATION CEREMONY!!

ゴチャ…
GOCHA
(MESSY?)

IT'S NOT RANDOM. I HAVE MY OWN METHOD.

I KEEP TELLING YOU TO NOT JUST STACK PAPERS AT RANDOM!!

イラ
IRA
(IRK)

ガサ
GASA
(RUMMAGE)

IRA

GOSO
(DIG)

GOSO

IRA

?

?

BASASA
(FLIP)
ぱさ

2 - C

I ABSOLUTELY HATE NAGISA TATSUMI!!

I HATE HER...

HISO ヒソ HISO ヒソ

But they seem so close.

You don't think...she's having a hard time with Tatsumi-san, do you?

HISO

We don't know how things really are, though.

HISO

HISO (PSST) ヒソ

Torayama-san looks tired...

HISO ヒソ

Being on the student council must be hard.

HISO ヒソ

HISO

ど

よ

ん

DOYON (GLOOM)

SHE DOESN'T SEEM LIKE SHE'D WORK WELL WITH A NICE PERSON LIKE TORAYAMA-SAN.

AND TATSUMI-SAN'S SO ALOOF...

THEY WERE ORIGINALLY COMPETING FOR THE SAME POSITION, AFTER ALL.

WHAT ABOUT SHIRAMINE-SAN?

YEAH, BUT... KUROSAWA-SAN'S KINDAAA...

KINDLY LEFT UNSAID

WHO ARE YOU?

SHE'D PROBABLY DO BETTER WITH ANOTHER COOL PERSON, LIKE KUROSAWA-SAN.

...I WONDER.

SHIRAMINE-SAN AND TORAYAMA-SAN ARE PRETTY SIMILAR...

MAYBE A KOUHAI WOULD BE BETTER ...?

EH? BUT...

MAYBE SHE JUST DOESN'T FIT WITH ANYONE?

HA
(GASP)

TIPS, HMM...?

AHEM.

DO YOU HAVE ANY TIPS ON HOW TO GET ALONG WITH HER?

YOU WERE IN THE SAME CLASS AS TATSUMI-SAN LAST YEAR TOO, RIGHT?

R-REALLY?

SHE HEARD US...

AH...

KAA
(BLUSH)

HUH?

HER LOCKER IS SURPRISINGLY MESSY...

TATSUMI-SAN IS PRETTY ALOOF, BUT SHE HAS HER APPROACHABLE MOMENTS TOO...

YOU FIND CLUTTER "APPROACHABLE"!?

HER HAIR IS ALWAYS SO NEAT, BUT EVERY NOW AND THEN...

...SHE'LL HAVE A BIT OF BED HEAD. IT'S SUPER CUTE...

I'M THE ONE WHO FIXES HER HAIR EVERY MORNING!!

I DON'T THINK...

...ANYONE ELSE HAS NOTICED THAT...

I KNOW THAT BETTER THAN ANYON—

NEVER MIND...

THIS SUCKS.

MROW.

IF I GOT WORKED UP OVER STUFF LIKE THAT, I'D LOOK JEALOUS.

AND THEN EVERYONE WOULD JUST KEEP THINKING WE'RE ACTUALLY FRIENDS...

THIS TOTALLY SUCKS!!!

IF YOU KNOW THAT, THEN DON'T DO IT.

YOU AREN'T GONNA YELL AT ME FOR LEAVING MY SOCKS AROUND?

ARE YOU NOT FEELING WELL?

VUU (BZZ) VUU

MOM, DAD...

...HURRY UP AND COME HOME...!!

I'M GETTING ATTACHED TO HER JUST BECAUSE WE LIVE TOGETHER.

Mom

MOM!!

GABA (JUMP)

Hikari.

How are things going with Nagisa-chan?

NOT TOO BAD...

Spring Year 1		About a year...
Original date.		
Spring Year 2		
...Stretch...		
Now	Spring Year 3	**A YEAR!?**
To here!?		
	Graduation	

About that...it looks like the job is going to take a little bit longer.

AGAIN? HOW LONG THIS TIME?

DO YOU KNOW WHEN YOU'RE COMING BACK?

NEVER MIND THAT. WHAT'S GOING ON?

114

So anyway, Hikari...

...maybe you should move into the Seiran dorms.

I'll contact the people at the dorm.

......

A year is a long time... and you're both going to be studying for entrance exams.

We can't just keep imposing.

CAN'T I STAY HERE?

...THAT'S REALLY SUDDEN...

BUT I'M HAPPY...

...I WANTED TO GO BACK HOME.

...JUST GETTING OUT OF THE TATSUMI HOUSE, AWAY FROM NAGISA...

Mom
Call Ended

GU
(CLENCH)

...OR RATHER, I SHOULD BE HAPPY.

SO WHY ...?

...GO SLEEP IN YOUR ROOM!!

NAGISA! IF YOU'RE GOING TO SLEEP...

HIKARI!

GACHA
(KACHAK)

...HEY, NAGISA.

IF I SAID...

...YOU'RE MOVING INTO THE DORM!?

MOM TOLD ME...

LONELI-NESS?

BUT WHY?

...THIS FEELING RIGHT NOW...

IF I HAD TO NAME...

THAT'S WHAT I THOUGHT TOO!

TORAYAMA-SAN!

SO THIS IS SUZURAN DORM...

SHIRA-MINE-SAN!

OH...

FOLLOW ME.

I THINK THAT'S BECAUSE I'LL BE YOUR ROOMMATE IF YOU DO MOVE IN.

SINCE MY CURRENT ROOMMATE IS A THIRD-YEAR.

KII (CREAK)

SO YOU'RE THE STUDENT GIVING ME THE TOUR?

YOU'RE HERE TO SEE THE DORM, RIGHT? I'LL SHOW YOU AROUND.

SHIRA-MINE-SAN, HUH...?

THIS IS THE CAFE-TERIA.

WE EAT BREAKFAST AND DINNER HERE.

I'M MAKING THINGS AWKWARD...

IF SHIRAMINE-SAN WERE THE VICE PRESIDENT...

YOU'RE REALLY BUSY, AND I'M TAKING UP YOUR TIME...

HEY, SHIRAMINE-SAN...I'M SORRY ABOUT THIS.

THIS IS THE BATH, AND THE LAUNDRY IS JUST NEXT DOOR...

SO
(BRUSH)

LET ME SHOW YOU AROUND.

I CAN JUST LOOK AROUND BY MYSELF...

SUZURAN DORM IS A NICE PLACE, SO I WANT TO HELP YOU SEE IT.

SHIRA-MINE-SAN...!!

YES, I THINK SO TOO.

WE'RE GOING TO MAKE GREAT FRIENDS!!

YOU'RE RIGHT!! THIS IS WHAT FRIENDS SHOULD BE LIKE!!

...LIVING HERE WITH SHIRAMINE-SAN WOULD BE SO MUCH BETTER...!!

OH HO HO!

AH HA HA!

INSTEAD OF LIVING WITH NAGISA...

HEY, SHIRAMINE-SAN.

WILL YOU HEAR ME OUT...?

...SO, YOU'RE NOT SURE WHETHER OR NOT YOU WANT TO MOVE INTO THE DORM?

I DON'T WANT TO BE HER FRIEND, BUT I STILL THINK I SHOULD BE AT HER SIDE...

I'M BEING A HYPOCRITE, AREN'T I?

...I JUST WANT TO HURRY UP AND MOVE INTO THE DORM.

...BUT LIVING WITH YOU WOULD BE A MILLION TIMES BETTER THAN LIVING WITH TATSUMI.

I WASN'T SURE...

WE AREN'T FRIENDS, THOUGH!

I'LL TELL YOU, BECAUSE YOU'RE YOU...

TATSUMI-SAN IS YOUR RIVAL, RIGHT?

WH-WHY DID YOU BRING UP KUROSAWA-SAN!?

DOESN'T IT BOTHER YOU THAT YOU AND KUROSAWA-SAN GET TREATED AS RIVALS?

...AND THINGS HAVE CHANGED IN TWO YEARS TOO.

WE'VE BOTH ENDED UP HELPING EACH OTHER.

W-WELL, I'VE THOUGHT ABOUT THIS A LOT...

EVEN IF WE STOP BEING RIVALS SOMEDAY...

...WE MIGHT EVENTUALLY SEE EYE-TO-EYE...

OH.

I'VE ONLY EVER CONSIDERED HER A RIVAL.

...DON'T THINK I COULD EVER BE FRIENDS WITH NAGISA.

I...

BUT JUST AS CLASSMATES, OF COURSE!!

EVEN IF YOU STOP BEING RIVALS...

HMM.

BUT... WE WERE ABLE TO BE HONEST WITH EACH OTHER BECAUSE WE WERE RIVALS.

AND I THINK I UNDERSTAND HER BETTER THAN ANYONE ELSE BECAUSE OF THAT TOO.

I DON'T THINK I FEEL THE WAY SHIRAMINE-SAN DOES...

IF THAT'S TRUE, WHAT I WANT IS—

...BUT I DON'T WANT TO LET ANYONE KNOW NAGISA BETTER THAN I DO.

...I WANT TO LIVE WITH NAGISA.

HUH!?

HIKARI, YOU...

WHY DO YOU FEEL THIS WAY?

HIKARI.

YOU CAN'T JUST DECIDE THAT ON YOUR OWN.

YOU'RE IMPOSING ON TATSUMI-SAN.

I REALIZED THAT I UNDERSTAND NAGISA BETTER...

...THAN ANYONE ELSE.

No Entrance

...I FELT REALLY LONELY.

WHEN YOU BROUGHT UP MOVING OUT OF THE TATSUMI HOUSEHOLD...

...WOULD
FEEL LIKE
A WASTE.

GOING
BACK TO
HOW IT WAS
BEFORE...

WE FINALLY
CAME TO AN
UNDER-
STANDING.

WELL...
YOU'RE
RIGHT.

AND IT
FEELS LIKE
I'D BE
LOSING AN
IMPORTANT
PIECE OF
ME.

...YEAH.

...THAT'S
WHY...

...I'M
GOING TO
BE HERE.

AUNTIE
...

...I REALLY WANT THIS TOO.

CAN HIKARI STAY WITH ME A LITTLE LONGER, PLEASE?

I THINK SO TOO!!

...I MEAN...

...LIVING TOGETHER MIGHT HELP US DEAL WITH STUDENT COUNCIL BUSINESS...

...THAT'S ALL.

が ば

GABA (JUMP)

YOU KNOW, FROM THAT PHONE CALL, I ALREADY THOUGHT MAYBE YOU DIDN'T WANT TO LEAVE...

...BUT WHEN DID YOU TWO GROW SO CLOSE?

!!

WE AREN'T FRIENDS!!

IF YOU JUST WANTED TO BE WITH YOUR FRIEND, THEN WHY NOT SAY SOOO?

GYAAA!

HEY, HIKARI, THOSE PAPERS ABOUT THE GYM...

SIGN: STUDENT COUNCIL ROOM

THE PRESIDENT IS ACTUALLY PRETTY SLOPPY...

THEY'RE AT IT AGAIN...

ALL I HAVE TO DO IS JUST ASK YOU.

HAVE YOU BEEN SLACKING EVEN MORE LATELY OR SOMETHING!?

THEY'RE ON THIS SHELF!!

I'LL ALWAYS HAVE SOMEONE HERE, WON'T I?

AND WHAT ARE YOU GOING TO DO IN THE FUTURE!?

HURRY AND CLEAN THIS UP!!

WHAT AM I GOING TO DO?

No way.

But I might not be here next year!!

Shut up!

I'll throw myself at you and beg you not to leave me alone.

EXCUSE ME!

I'M HERE FROM THE VOLLEY-BALL TEAM.

COME ON. LET'S GO.

...OH, FINE.

I'LL STICK WITH YOU A BIT LONGER.

134

In the Conference Room

NODOKA
HIGH SCHOOL SECOND-YEAR. LIVES IN THE DORM BECAUSE HER HOUSE IS FAR AWAY.

AKEMI
HIGH SCHOOL SECOND-YEAR. NODOKA'S GIRLFRIEND.

OH, YEAH... BECAUSE SENOO-SENPAI IS LEAVING.

I HEAR SHE'S GOING TO MOVE IN WITH SHIRAMINE-SAN.

THANK YOU.

OH!

TORAYAMA-SAN CAME TO VISIT THE DORM?

PITO (FLOP)

AND IT MEANS WE CAN BOTH STAY IN THE SAME ROOM TOO.

YEAH, IT IS.

THEY DON'T USUALLY CHANGE ROOM ASSIGNMENTS, SO IT'S REALLY EASY TO FIGURE THINGS LIKE THAT OUT. IT'S NICE!

OH... BUT...

...WILL THEY MAKE US SWITCH ROOMS IF THEY FIND OUT WE'RE DATING?

IF YOU'RE WORRIED, THEN MAYBE QUIT BEING SO OBVIOUS.

✳ *Ayaka Shiramine* ✳

Ayaka Shiramine

Second-year student at Seiran Academy High School. An honors student who hates to lose and Yurine Kurosawa's rival. She's known as the model Seiran student, to the point that everyone around her wanted her to be student council president. She was able to rethink her relationship with her mother because of Kurosawa's advice, but she still hasn't been able to assert her independence.

SO, TORAYAMA-SAN, RIGHT? SHE'S NOT MOVING INTO THE DORM?

LOOKS LIKE IT.

...I WAS HOPING SOMEONE WOULD COME ALONG WHO COULD DEAL WITH AYAKA-CHAN WHEN SHE ACTS LIKE THIS.

BUT I GUESS THAT'S NOT HAPPENING...

FUU (SIGH)

STOP TALKING TO YOURSELF AND GET READY.

YOU LEAVE TOMORROW!!

YOUR FAMILY TRIP IS... TO HAWAII, RIGHT?

YEAH.

WE'RE ONLY GOING FOR A WEEK THIS TIME, THOUGH.

I'LL BE GRADU-ATING SOON...

...AND I WON'T BE HERE TO LISTEN TO YOUR TROUBLES.

SO CALL A FRIEND IF ANYTHING HAPPENS, OKAY?

MAYBE KUROSAWA-SAN...?

MUST BE NICE TO CONTINUE ON TO OUR SCHOOL'S UNIVERSITY.

HUH!!?

I DON'T EVEN KNOW HER NUMBER.

WHY, DID YOU THINK I HAD THAT?

BESIDES, I DON'T HAVE A CELLPHONE.

I HAVE NO REASON TO GET A HOLD OF HER IN THE FIRST PLACE!!

ツン (TSUN) (FWIP)

WHA...? THEN HOW... DO YOU NORMALLY GET A HOLD OF HER AND STUFF?

PON (GRAB)

HUH!?

GO GET KUROSAWA-SAN'S NUMBER TOMORROW.

...WHY DO I...

...NEED KUROSAWA-SAN'S NUMBER ANYWAY...?

'MORNING, SHIRAMINE-SAN!

'M-MORNING.

GUNUNU (GRRRR)

ASK HER RIGHT AWAY, FIRST THING IN THE MORNING!!

JUST ASK HER BEFORE YOU CAN START MAKING EXCUSES ABOUT IT!!

BA (WHAM)

KURO-SAWA-SAN!!

BUN (SHAKE)

BUN

140

KAA
(BLUSH)
かぁ…

CAN
I...

CAN?

Um...

Can...

もじ…
MOJI
(FIDGET)

'MORNING!!

...AN
GET
OUR
—?

WAAA
(WHOOSH)

THAT'S WHY YOU TWO NEED TO HELP OUT TOO!!

THE FULL MOON IS GOING TO LOOK ABSOLUTELY HUGE.

BUT IT'S SUPPOSED TO SNOW ALL DAY TODAY.

I KNOW!

...IT'S FINE, UEHARA-SAN...

HUH?
WERE YOU TWO IN THE MIDDLE OF SOMETHING?

Super Moon

HEY, HAVE YOU HEARD? THERE'S GONNA BE A SUPER MOON TONIGHT!

141

Kurosawa-san is helping Uehara-san make good weather charms.

Uehara-san gathered her friends to make a whole bunch of them...

!!BOWED OUT...

When are you going to ask for her number?

IT'S ALREADY LUNCH-TIME!

...So? ☆

CAME TO SEE HOW IT WENT →

HAA (SIGH)

AND I DON'T LIKE YOUR ATTITUDE!!

I don't even need it in the first place! Honestly!!

GEEZ...

HOW CAN YOU MESS THINGS UP THIS BADLY?

WE AREN'T EVEN ALL THAT CLOSE TO BEGIN WITH.

I MEAN, YES, I THOUGHT WE'D COME TO AN UNDER-STANDING...

...THAT ALL THE TIME I SPENT WORKING SO DESPERATELY HARD WAS WORTH IT.

I THINK I WANT TO PROVE...

...WHAT DOES THAT SAY ABOUT MY CONVICTION?

...AND SETTLE FOR BEING FRIENDLY INSTEAD...

IF I CAN'T BEAT HER...

AND BE HONEST WITH YOURSELF?

BEAT HER, AND...

I JUST WANT TO BEAT HER SOON.

...DON'T SAY IT LIKE I'M SOME CHILD.

...WERE YOU STALKING ME?

WANT TO WALK BACK TOGETHER?

IT FELT LIKE YOU HAD SOMETHING TO SAY THIS MORNING.

PAN (FWAP)

...IT'S NOTHING.

I SAID IT'S NOTHING!!

REALLY?

SAKU

SAKU

SAKU

SAKU (CRUNCH)

SAKU

EVEN THOUGH WE MADE A LOT OF WEATHER CHARMS...

...SPEAKING OF THE THOSE...

THE SNOW ISN'T STOPPING, IS IT?

YEAH.

THERE WAS ONE PARTICULARLY ODD... I MEAN...

...UNIQUE ONE HANGING UP.

GLAD TO KNOW I WAS RIGHT.

I WAS DYING TO CONFIRM BUT COULDN'T ASK ANYONE ELSE.

I KNEW IT.

WHAAA, I CAN'T MAKE IT CUTE!

AH HA HA!

THAT WAS KOUNO-SAN'S.

...SORRY, THIS IS PRETTY BORING, ISN'T IT?

NO.

I...

...WANTED TO TALK ABOUT SILLY STUFF WITH YOU.

...IT'D BE COOL TO BE ABLE TO TELL YOU ABOUT THEM RIGHT ON THE SPOT.

I WAS THINKING, IF I SEE REALLY PRETTY STARS IN THE MIDDLE OF THE NIGHT...

YOU WERE REALLY BUSY UNTIL JUST RECENTLY, AFTER ALL.

146

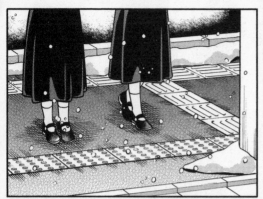

...OR REALLY BIG AND BEAUTIFUL...

...WERE REALLY MIS-SHAPEN TONIGHT...

IF THE MOON...

IF THE STARS WERE REALLY PRETTY...

HMM.

BUT RIGHT NOW IT'S SNOWING.

IF SHE DECIDED SHE WANTED TO TELL ME ABOUT STUFF LIKE THAT...

...I THINK...

...IT MIGHT MAKE ME HAPPY...

WOULD THAT MAKE YOU HAPPY TOO?

WELL, SEE YOU TOMORROW.

WOULD IT?

148

BIKU
(FLINCH)

THE FULL MOON TONIGHT!!

YOU MADE ALL THOSE CHARMS BECAUSE YOU WANTED TO SEE IT, DIDN'T YOU?

I DON'T THINK WE SHOULD LET EVERYONE'S HARD WORK GO TO WASTE...!!

THE MOON?

OH...WHAT UEHARA-SAN SAID.

I'LL TELL YOU IF I CAN SEE IT FROM THE DORM!!

SO I'D LIKE...

...TO GET...

...YOUR PHONE NUMBER.

OKAY.

150

CALL ME ANYTIME.

ARE YOU SURE ABOUT THIS!?

I'LL ONLY CALL IF SOMETHING HAPPENS, YOU KNOW!!

I...

IT'S OKAY.

SORRY. I KEPT YOU WAITING TOO LONG.

BURORO (VROOM)

PA (SHINE)

OH!

...WILL YOU WAIT FOR THE NEXT LIGHT WITH ME?

...OH, FINE.

Mizuki Senoo

WHEN YOU'RE LIVING IN A DORM, YOU CAN GO TO THE DORM MOTHER IF YOU NEED SOMETHING.

STILL...

SHE'S SUCH A WORRY-WART.

I HAVE A BAD FEELING ABOUT THIS.

JUST GO!

I FINALLY GOT MIZUKI ON HER WAY.

THAT'S A LOAD OFF MY MIND.

KON (KNOCK)

A CALL FOR YOU.

THE DORM MOTHER'S LOOKING FOR YOU.

GACHA (KACHAK)

KON

SHIRA-MINE-SAN!

HELLO?

IS IT KUROSAWA-SAN?

Hello?

Ayaka?

VUVUVU
(BZZZ)

Suzuran Do...

WHAT IS IT?
THE SNOW
STOPPED,
BUT THE
MOON ISN'T
OUT YET...

GABA
(JUMP)

HELLO?
SHIRAMINE-
SAN?

Kurosawa-
san...

It's
nothing.

?

153

KO
(CLINK)

KOTSUN
(CLACK)

KOTSUN

KARARA
(SLIDE)

KOTSUN

......SNFF
......

I CAME TO SEE YOU!

SO BE QUIET AND COME WITH ME.

...I'M NOT ACTUALLY SUPPOSED TO LET NON-RESIDENTS IN, YOU KNOW.

I CAME HERE ONCE BEFORE.

...I'M SURPRISED YOU KNEW WHICH ONE WAS MY ROOM.

THE BACK DOOR IS THIS WAY.

......

OKAY.

SO... WHAT'S WRONG?

...MY MOM TOLD ME TO COME BACK.

IT'S NOT SO FAR THAT I WOULDN'T BE ABLE TO GO TO SCHOOL HERE ANYMORE.

WON'T THAT MEAN YOU'RE MUCH FARTHER AWAY?

...LEAVE THE DORM AND MOVE HOME?

...AND I WANTED TO AVOID MY MOM AS MUCH AS POSSIBLE.

I JUST... THOUGHT IT WAS A WASTE TO SPEND SO MUCH TIME COMMUTING...

AND MOM SAID NO MATTER HOW HARD I TRY HERE, I'M NEVER GOING TO GET BETTER ANYWAY.

BUT MIZUKI WON'T BE HERE ANYMORE NEXT YEAR...

...SO OF COURSE SHE'D SAY THAT.

I HAVEN'T PRODUCED ANY RESULTS...

I DIDN'T HAVE A RESPONSE OR ANYTHING...

I DON'T WANT TO LOSE IT.

BUT... THIS IS THE ONLY PLACE WHERE I BELONG.

SHE'S JUST WORRIED ABOUT ME.

WHAT AM I SUPPOSED TO DO?

BE NUMBER ONE, SHIRAMINE-SAN!

...THEN YOU CAN SAY WHATEVER YOU WANT TO YOUR MOM!!

TAKE ME DOWN DURING THIS TERM'S FINAL EXAMS AND TAKE THE NUMBER ONE SPOT...

...BUT...

I DON'T KNOW IF YOU'LL BE ABLE TO COME TO A COMPLETE UNDER-STANDING...

BUT WILL SHE ACTUALLY LISTEN...?

YOU'RE... PROBABLY RIGHT.

THAT'S GOTTA BE WAY MORE EFFECTIVE THAN SAYING ANYTHING AS YOU ARE.

158

I HAVE TO GET GOING NOW.

WE HAVE SCHOOL IN THE MORNING, AND I DIDN'T BRING ANYTHING WITH ME.

UM.

I'M SORRY... FOR CALLING AND MAKING YOU WORRY.

IT'S FINE.

...KURO-SAWA-SAN.

WHY DO YOU DO SO MUCH FOR ME?

...BECAUSE ...

...I APPRECIATE YOU.

......

BECAUSE I...

OH!

KII
(CREAK)

I WONDER IF UEHARA-SAN AND THE OTHERS SAW THIS.

H-HEY!!

...WELL, I GUESS I DID MAKE HER COME OVER TONIGHT.

I'LL LET IT SLIDE.

HMPH!

JUST HOW MUCH I APPRECIATE HER...

I GOT IT ACROSS TO HER THIS TIME, RIGHT?

I'LL BEAT HER AND TELL MOM EVERYTHING I HAVE TO SAY...

...AND THEN...

...I WANT TO BEAT HER.

I HAVE TO BEAT HER.

BECAUSE I—

WHY DO YOU DO SO MUCH FOR ME?

BECAUSE I LIKE YOU.

IT'S NOT LIKE IT'S WEIRD TO SAY THAT.

MAYBE IF I CAN BE NORMAL...

...I CAN BE MORE CONFIDENT.

I WONDER IF EVEN NORMAL GIRLS WOULD WORRY ABOUT THIS.

IF THERE'S ANYTHING THAT I'M LACKING...

...I THINK IT'S CONFIDENCE.

NANAE
MIDDLE SCHOOL FIRST-YEAR. DOESN'T EXACTLY COME FROM A SNOWY REGION.

 MACHI
MIDDLE SCHOOL FIRST-YEAR. COMES FROM A SNOWY REGION.

Snowy Day

KISS THEATER: WHAT'S BEHIND THE STORY!? ✳ PEOPLE OTHER THAN THE MAIN CHARACTERS HAVE STORIES TOO. HERE, WE PRESENT THE "LITTLE LOVE" STORIES HAPPENING BEHIND THE SCENES.

Kiss and White Lily for My Dearest Girl
Side Stories

HEY.

WANT TO JOIN THE STUDENT COUNCIL?

ARMBAND: STUDENT COUNCIL

...WHO ARE YOU?

The Student Council: Prelude ★

THINK OF ME AS THE NEXT STUDENT COUNCIL PRESIDENT!

I'M HASE, A SECOND-YEAR.

I'M SECRETARY ON THE STUDENT COUNCIL RIGHT NOW.

I'VE BEEN LOOKING FOR CANDIDATES, AND I THINK YOU'D BE GOOD.

I'M LOOKING FOR TALENTED FIRST-YEARS WHO'D BE WILLING TO DO THE JOB.

...FOR ODD JOBS, I GUESS?

WE NEED NEXT YEAR'S STUDENT COUNCIL ASSISTANTS...

IF YOU JOIN NOW, YOU'LL BE ON THE FAST TRACK TO FUTURE PRESIDENT, YOU KNOW.

WELL?

WOULD YOU BE WILLING TO WORK UNDER ME?

......

OH!

AN IMMEDIATE ANSWER!

YES.

YES, I'D LIKE TO DO IT.

I ALSO BELIEVE I'M SOMEONE WHO SHOULD BE STUDENT COUNCIL PRESIDENT.

SIGN: STUDENT COUNCIL ROOM

I'M JUST GONNA INTRODUCE YOU TO THE OTHER MEMBERS TODAY, OKAY?

生徒会室

INTER-ESTING.

NICE!

GA (GRAB)

I HAVE NO CLUE WHAT IS BETWEEN YOU GUYS...

...BUT I NEED YOU, TATSUMI-SAN!!

YOU TWO MIGHT COME TO ACCEPT EACH OTHER AS YOU DO YOUR WORK FOR THE STUDENT COUNCIL!!

WELL...

I'LL HELP!!

IF YOU INSIST, SENPAI...

THAT COULD EASILY BE TAKEN THE WRONG WAY...

cafe

THAT SAID...

AH-HA-HA- HA-HA!

...THOSE TWO JUST NEVER DID GET ALONG!

SHE WAS MORE LIKE A STRAY DOG, THOUGH.

THAT RANDOM STUFF YOU BLURTED OUT ACTUALLY WORKED.

TATSUMI-SAN DID GET PRETTY ATTACHED TO YOU, HASE-SAN.

WELL, EVEN IF I DIDN'T KNOW, IT WAS ME WHO BROUGHT HER IN—

THAT NEVER HAPPENS.

STILL... I CAN'T BELIEVE YOU WILLINGLY STEPPED INTO AN ANNOYING SITUATION LIKE THAT.

WOULDN'T IT BE FASTER TO JUST APPLY THAT TO YOUR WORK?

ANYTHING!

BESIDES, I'LL DO ANYTHING IF IT MEANS I CAN SLACK OFF MORE!

1-C

THANKS FOR HELPING OUT, RYOU-CHAN.

IT'S NOTHING... THIS IS FUN.

I KNEW YOU WERE IN THE VOLUNTEER CLUB, AMANE-SAN...

CHIRA
(GLANCE)

YEAH, YEAH! WE'RE GOING TO THROW A CHRISTMAS PARTY AT THE LOCAL PRESCHOOL!

YOU'RE MAKING THESE FOR THE VOLUNTEER CLUB, RIGHT?

I SEE...

NINA'S REALLY NICE!

WH— WHAT?

...BUT I DIDN'T EXPECT NINA-SAN TO BE.

I'M NOT ALL THAT INTERESTED IN VOLUNTEERING.

I'LL JUST KEEP THAT TO MYSELF...

NOT THAT I HAVE ALL THAT MANY MEMORIES OF HER BEING NICE...

I'M JUST HERE BECAUSE AMANE IS.

SHE ACTS SCARY...

...BUT SHE REALLY IS A GOOD PERSON.

SHE'S ACTUALLY ... KIND...

GATA (CLATTER)

SORRY, I HAVE TO GO.

0.00

YEAH, BUT...

AND SHE JUST UP AND DIS-APPEARS ...

SHE DOESN'T FINISH HER LUNCH.

SHE'S ALWAYS LOOKING AT THE CLOCK.

DON'T YOU THINK NINA-SAN'S BEEN WEIRD LATELY...?

AMANE-SAN'S RIGHT.

I SHOULDN'T PRY...

YEAH, I GUESS...

...I'M SURE SHE'LL TELL US WHY WHEN SHE'S READY.

ささみ 子ネコ用

CAN: CHICKEN KITTEN FOOD

ドキ

DOKI (BADMP)

ドキ

DOKI

I'M PRETTY SURE THAT STOREROOM IS UNUSED.

WHAT IN THE WORLD ...?

ドキ

DOKI

ガラ

DOKI

GARA (SLIDE)

!?

THERE ARE A BUNCH OF CANS OF CAT FOOD ON THE GROUND!?

MEW.

BAG: DISPOSABLE LITTER MATS

I THOUGHT YOU WERE ACTING A BIT WEIRD LATELY...

Y—

YOU'RE KEEPING A CAT AT SCHOOL ...!?

BASAAA (FLAP)

HEY!!

KEEP IT DOWN!!

SHE WAS CRYING BECAUSE SHE WAS HUNGRY, AND I COULDN'T LEAVE HER...

MROW!

I DIDN'T WANT TO DRAG YOU TWO INTO THIS...

AT THE END OF THE DAY, THIS IS MY RESPONSIBILITY.

FUWA (YAWN)

I CAN'T KEEP HER AT THE DORM...BUT I GOT ATTACHED TO HER.

I LOOKED ONLINE FOR SOMEONE TO TAKE HER, BUT I COULDN'T FIND ANYONE.

RIGHT...

I MIGHT HAVE MADE THINGS EVEN WORSE...

BUT YOU KNOW YOU CAN'T KEEP THIS UP, RIGHT?

THAT WORKS!!

I'M SO RELIEVED!

...!

LET'S HAVE THE VOLUNTEER CLUB FIND SOMEONE TO TAKE HER.

SHUN (DROOP)

179

KOSO
(PSST)

SEE?

NINA'S REALLY NICE, RIGHT?

YEAH...

......

HA HA HA...

I JUST WISH SHE'D BE AS NICE TO ME AS SHE IS TO THE CAT...

AFTERWORD

I WAS THINKING HOW ONE OF THE GOOD THINGS ABOUT RIVALRIES IS THAT THEY CAN HAPPEN EVEN IF YOU CAN'T DEAL WITH THE OTHER PERSON'S PERSONALITY. (GREETINGS.) HELLO, CANNO HERE.

ONCE AGAIN, THANK YOU SO MUCH TO EVERYONE IN THE *ALIVE* EDITORIAL DEPARTMENT; THE DESIGNER SEKI-SAN; YUI-SAN, WHO WAS SO HELPFUL; MY FAMILY; MY FRIENDS; AND EVERYONE WHO CHEERED ME ON (WHETHER FROM THE PAGE OR THE SCREEN) ALL THE WAY TO VOLUME 8 AND WHO HELPED GET THIS BOOK OUT SUCCESSFULLY. THANKS TO ALL OF YOU, I THINK I CAN SEE WHERE SHIRAMINE AND KUROSAWA ARE HEADED NOW. I'M PLANNING ON HAVING VOLUME 9 BE MORE SHIRAMINE/KUROSAWA. I'LL DO MY BEST.

THANK YOU SO MUCH FOR READING THIS FAR! I HOPE TO SEE YOU AGAIN IN THE NEXT VOLUME.

CANNO

I DIDN'T HAVE AS MANY CHANCES TO DRAW THEM IN THEIR HOME CLOTHES AS I THOUGHT I WOULD, SO HERE...

YURI EXPO 2018

I'M GOING TO BE PARTICIPATING WITH SOME MAIN VISUALS AND MERCH. PLEASE CHECK IT OUT!

Kiss & White Lily for My Dearest Girl

8

{ CANNO }

TRANSLATION: LEIGHANN HARVEY
LETTERING: ALEXIS ECKERMAN

ANOKO NI KISS TO SHIRAYURI WO Vol. 8
©Canno 2018
First published in Japan in 2018 by KADOKAWA CORPORATION, Tokyo.
English translation rights arranged with KADOKAWA CORPORATION, Tokyo
through Tuttle-Mori Agency, Inc., Tokyo.

English translation © 2019 by Yen Press, LLC

Yen Press
1290 Avenue of the Americas
New York, NY 10104

Visit us at yenpress.com
facebook.com/yenpress
twitter.com/yenpress
yenpress.tumblr.com
instagram.com/yenpress

First Yen Press Edition: March 2019

Yen Press is an imprint of Yen Press, LLC.
The Yen Press name and logo are trademarks of Yen Press, LLC.

The publisher is not responsible for websites (or their content)
that are not owned by the publisher.

Library of Congress Control Number: 2016958499

ISBNs: 978-1-9753-0214-6 (paperback)
978-1-9753-0390-7 (ebook)

10 9 8 7 6 5 4 3 2 1

WOR

Printed in the United States of America